# LittleBIG Planet™

## Ultimate Official Guidebook

GROSSET & DUNLAP
An Imprint of Penguin Group (USA) Inc.

D1308593

# Before You Get Started

- **Sit a safe distance from the screen**
- **Play in a well-lit environment**
- **Take regular breaks for fifteen minutes every hour**
- **When playing online, never give out your actual name or any other personal details**
- **Respect other players**
- **Have fun!**

GROSSET & DUNLAP
Published by the Penguin Group
Penguin Group (USA) Inc., 375 Hudson Street, New York, New York 10014, USA
Penguin Group (Canada), 90 Eglinton Avenue East, Suite 700, Toronto, Ontario M4P 2Y3, Canada
(a division of Pearson Penguin Canada Inc.)
Penguin Books Ltd., 80 Strand, London WC2R 0RL, England
Penguin Group Ireland, 25 St. Stephen's Green, Dublin 2, Ireland
(a division of Penguin Books Ltd.)
Penguin Group (Australia), 250 Camberwell Road, Camberwell, Victoria 3124, Australia
(a division of Pearson Australia Group Pty. Ltd.)
Penguin Books India Pvt. Ltd., 11 Community Centre, Panchsheel Park, New Delhi—110 017, India
Penguin Group (NZ), 67 Apollo Drive, Rosedale, Auckland 0632, New Zealand
(a division of Pearson New Zealand Ltd.)
Penguin Books (South Africa) (Pty.) Ltd., 24 Sturdee Avenue,
Rosebank, Johannesburg 2196, South Africa

Penguin Books Ltd., Registered Offices: 80 Strand, London WC2R 0RL, England

ISBN 978-0-448-45762-8          10 9 8 7 6 5 4 3 2 1

# Welcome!

"Planet Earth, or as the rest of the omniverse calls it, the Orb of Dreamers. The occupants of which spend so much time asleep and dreaming, their vast imaginations humming away, charged with creative energy. Where does it all go? Up through a cerebral-bilical cord where it collects and melds with all the other dreamers' energies, and something wonderful happens—it forms a world. An ethereal dreamscape of adventure and possibilities; an abstract plane of beautiful wonderment, just waiting to be explored. And you can go there."

Welcome to the *LittleBigPlanet Ultimate Official Guidebook*, the essential guide to help you unlock the secrets of your own Sackboy or Sackgirl's LittleBig world. Discover hidden levels, out-of-reach treasures, and use the items you collect on your journey to create new and exciting adventures to play with your friends or share online.

# Contents

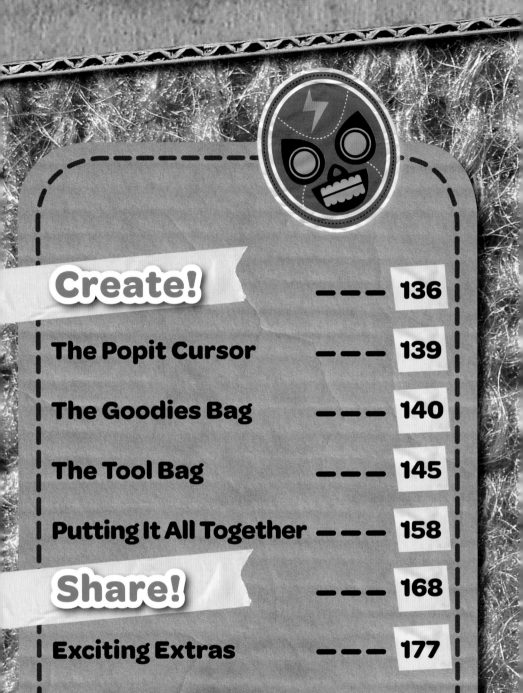

# Your Sack Person

The first person you meet in LittleBigPlanet will be your Sack Person. This cute, little thing is your link to this mysterious, new world, so take the time to familiarize yourself with his or her controls before you begin your journey. Soon you'll be snarling at your enemies, dancing for joy when you solve that difficult puzzle, and maybe even taking a break to play a little air guitar along the way!

## The Controls

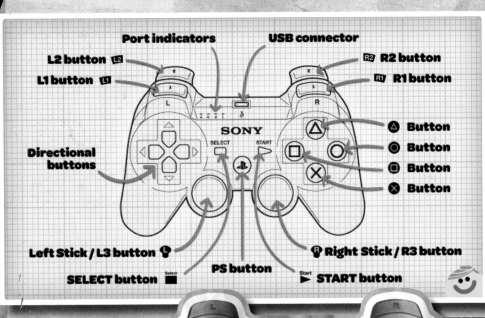

Port indicators    USB connector

L2 button  L2          R2 button  R2
L1 button  L1          R1 button  R1

Directional buttons          △ Button
                             ⊙ Button
SELECT    START               ▣ Button
SONY                          ⊗ Button

Left Stick / L3 button  L        R  Right Stick / R3 button
SELECT button  Select    PS button    Start  START button

## The Start Menu

While in a level, the Start Menu lets you choose to restart the level or return to the Pod. If you are online, you can check any LittleBigPlanet messages you may have received as well as check on your friends' progress. From here you can also replay any tutorial videos and voice-overs you've heard during the game so far, just in case you need to refresh your memory!

## The Good Grief! Menu

Everybody wants to enjoy LittleBigPlanet in a clean and safe environment, so if you see anything that shouldn't be there, this is the menu where you can report it.

## The Popit Menu

You'll use your Popit a lot, as it holds all the tools you need to customize both your Sack Person and the world around you. Press ■ to open it, and from there you'll find menus for stickers and decorations, customizing your character, retrying when you get stuck, and a nifty little text chat option that creates a speech bubble over your head. There is also a "Hearted" page where you can store all your favorite items from the other menus. To add them, simply press the ● button when over an item you like and then press "Heart."

**7**

## Your Pod

Your Pod is a cross between your bedroom and your first shed, and it is from here that you'll navigate the world of LittleBigPlanet. It might look like a bare cardboard shell when you first arrive, but once you've explored the worlds outside your window, you'll be able to decorate your Pod with the stickers and objects you've collected on your travels and turn it into a unique home away from home for your Sack Person.

The Wireless Controller in the back of the Pod is your computer. You can use it to navigate the planets below. Press ■ to access it, and choose from one of the three worlds outside.

## LittleBigPlanet

This is the main story mode of the game. From here you can play the various kingdoms you've unlocked both online and alone, Quick Play with other Sack People online, or explore user-created levels. There's even an option to buy extra costumes and theme packs from the LittleBigPlanet Store.

Once you've completed the first three levels of Story, you'll also have access to two other moons.

Story

The Wilderness
By The Collector

100%
Goodies & prizes won

### The Info Moon

The Info Moon summarizes your progress through the game and lets you tailor your online avatar and pictures. You can also use this moon to see how the other players on your friends list are doing, as well as check out the latest news on the LittleBigPlanet blog.

### My Moon

Here is where you create your own LittleBigPlanet levels, filled with new puzzles and challenges to put up online for other players to check out and rate.

### The PlayStation Eye

If you're lucky enough to possess a PlayStation Eye camera and have it hooked up to your console, you can use it to create personalized pictures and stickers to place around the levels. In the Popit menu, scroll across the Stickers section until you reach the camera page, where you can choose frames and shapes to customize your picture.

# Play!

It's time to get started on your journey of wild imagination! Take the time to wander through the introduction and meet all the lovely people that made the game before visiting the tranquil Gardens. There, you'll meet the first citizens of this world. These friendly folks will help you on your way, giving you tips about what lies ahead and maybe even asking you for a favor or two.

It's not all fun and games, though, as some of the kingdoms you'll be exploring might not be as welcoming as others. Something is happening to LittleBigPlanet, and you have arrived just in time. The LittleBig people are disappearing, and while the Creator Curators are tasked with defending their own kingdoms, it'll be up to you to solve the mystery of the Collector . . .

## Tutorials

As you wander through the introduction you'll discover the first of many tutorials. These helpful little televisions will tell you all you need to know about customizing your characters, making them move or change moods, and, well, everything really. Remember, if you need a reminder on how to do any of the things you learn along the way, you can always replay the video or voice-over from the Start Menu.

**THE KING**

# The Gardens: First Steps

The first kingdom you encounter on your voyage through LittleBigPlanet is the Gardens, overseen by The King and Queen Creator Curators. The King's Garden is the perfect place to practice the controls you learned in the introduction, and helpful tutorials are dotted around the level to teach you the finer points of jumping, adding stickers, collecting items, and using the PlayStation Eye.

Along the way you'll meet Dumpty (whose body hides a wealth of score bubbles), navigate a deadly waterwheel, and attempt to escape a collapsing bridge!

## *Tricky Challenges*

-------------------------------------------------------

Generously, The King hasn't charged you with navigating anything too difficult for your first outing in his kingdom, but to get all those extra score bubbles, it's worth risking your life to jump from spoke to spoke on the waterwheel.

The Queen will demonstrate how to use the stickers you receive to dress King Henry so that he can lower the bridge for you to continue. Don't forget to press **[R3]** to flip the **Shoe Sticker** over for his left foot, though! You can also use stickers to decorate your Sack Person. While in the stickers section, use **[L1]** or **[R1]** to rotate your Sack Person and place a sticker or photo anywhere on its outfit or head!

Halfway through the level you might get a small scare when a bridge you are crossing collapses, dropping you to the bottom of a deep pit. But don't worry, there is a helpful tutorial showing you how to use the "retry" button in your Popit to escape such impossible situations.

13

Joyous greetings and welcome to my gardens. I created them with a little help from my wife, The Queen. Now a big adventure awaits you. Good luck!

◉ Close

## Favorite Items

First Steps contains lots of items to get you started with customizing your own Sack Person. In amongst the Elizabethan outfits given to you by Dumpty, you'll find a rather hilarious **Fancy Moustache**, and for completing the level you'll receive a **Big Kiss Costume**. Whoever has given your Sack Person such a big smacker is anybody's guess, but our money is on The Queen!

**The Gardens**

## Secret Gifts

If you play through this level again, you will notice a sticker switch near the beginning, on top of the first wall. Use the **Rainbow Shoe** sticker you picked up at the beginning of the level to unlock a race mode! Not only will this increase your maximum score, but it will also lower a bird on a wire above the collapsing bridge. If you manage to jump and grab the bird, you can swing across and complete the level without dying and collect the **Pirate Hook** and **Eye Patch** at the end of the level!

# The Gardens:
## Get a Grip

Get a Grip is all about grabbing and pulling, so you'll be using **[R1]** a lot early on to drag blocks and ramps around to navigate obstacles. As you make your way through the Gardens, you'll discover the wooden steeds. These beasts can carry you quickly down the steep slopes of the level—but watch your balance! About halfway through you'll have to start grabbing onto the swinging sponge balls to avoid dying, then quickly run and jump from seesaw to seesaw to get to the top of the hill before the final race to the finish line!

## Tricky Challenges

The seesaw puzzles take a bit of getting used to, but a few practices should have you timing those jumps perfectly before the balance tips again.

The level itself is not too difficult to navigate, but if you want to find all the hidden items, you need to think carefully about whether the sponge balls or fabric blocks can be used to swing or climb into the treetops before moving on to the next section.

When racing down hills on your horse, be sure to grab onto the foam sections to keep your balance, especially if you're trying to beat the timer. But watch out for any sticker switches and objects that you might pass along the way so that you can go back for them.

## Favorite Items

There are a lot of **Golden Star Sticker** switches in this level, and you'll need to play the next level to the end to retrieve them. But it's worth going back and replaying Get a Grip because it unlocks an awful lot of goodies.

To gain the **Soccer Ball Object,** you need to slap the **Star Sticker** and the **Teapot Sticker** (which is lying handily nearby) on the switches by the first checkpoint to trigger the items to drop to the ground. And if you get to the treetops near the seesaws, you can unlock the rather nifty **Eye Spring Object** the same way.

There are plenty of other **Star Sticker** switches around, so keep walking along the treetops and jump onto the clouds for some celestial rewards. Finally, jump off your final steed mid-race to get the **Crowd Object** the same way.

## Secret Gifts

Even if you are convinced you have found all the items in the level, here are a couple you will almost definitely have missed!

Get the **Sun Doodle Sticker** that lies behind the checkpoint in the middle of the tree trunk, about halfway through the level, by moving onto the rear plane on the left-hand side of the root.

The same trick works on The Queen. Go behind her to find the hidden **Black Crown Outline Sticker**.

# The Gardens:

# Skate to Victory

Right from the beginning, The King warns you that the easy times are over and this is where it gets serious! Hitching a ride on a convenient bird, you make your way into the entrance of a haunted castle via some fast-moving windmills. Before you go in, take the time to learn about the fun Camera Tool before donning a jetpack and using the foam balls to lower the drawbridge. Once inside, you'll be avoiding stomping boots and dodging ghosts as you pull blocks and leap platforms to open trapdoors. Actually, the boots are your friends and, combined with a well-timed jump, can kick you into hard-to-reach areas to gain a few more prize bubbles. Thankfully, Dumpty is waiting to greet you at the top of the castle to give you a bit of fun before the level ends. Give his skateboard a good push and hold on tight as you race down the hill to the finish line!

## Tricky Challenges

If you want to finish the level without dying and complete that **Pirate Costume** you've been working toward, you're going to have to be careful of the ghosts. Take your time to learn their movements as they will often swing back and forth as well as side to side, and don't be afraid to jump over them.

Have fun with the skateboard race at the end—you'll soon figure out that hanging onto different areas of the board as well as moving along it while airborne can change your flight path. This will come in useful during the mini level later!

## Favorite Items

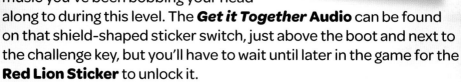

It's time to grab some of that lovely music you've been bobbing your head along to during this level. The ***Get it Together* Audio** can be found on that shield-shaped sticker switch, just above the boot and next to the challenge key, but you'll have to wait until later in the game for the **Red Lion Sticker** to unlock it.

An easy item now: The **Skateboard Object** is a lot of fun to play with in your own custom levels, so grab it here among The Queen's stash at the end of the level.

## Secret Gifts

Left over from the Get a Grip level, there are a couple of **Golden Star Sticker** switches. Go left when you start the level to fill those mini teacups with gifts. And use your jetpack to get into the treetops for the final **Star Sticker** switch for some tree-related objects.

There are some not-so-secret-but-hard-to-get items on a ledge near the last windmill in this level. Time the release of your grip carefully to fling yourself onto the ledge. You only have to touch it for a minute before the whole thing comes tumbling down to the bottom of the pit where you can easily collect the items. (There is also another rotating star puzzle down there as well!)

For those who want a real challenge, use the rising blocks near the 2x player section to jump over the ghost and onto the ledge of items above. There is a secret room on the left with a **Star Sticker** switch and a host of items to collect as a result.

# The Gardens: Mini Levels

## Castle Climb

Grab the challenge key for this mini level near the Little One on Get a Grip by running up the seesaw and swinging on the foam ball.

This challenge is a difficult one to start with, and you may find yourself plummeting back to the beginning again. The trick is not to rush; make sure the seesaws have fully tilted before running and jumping to the top. It will make it easier to reach the ledges and foam balls at the top.

After navigating the seesaws and spikes to get to the top, you'll be confronted with a series of clouds hovering above an expanse of spikes—keep moving and don't grab onto the clouds or else you will get flipped to your death as they tilt.

## Tie Skipping

Grab the challenge key next to the **Red Lion Sticker** puzzle in Skate to Victory to unlock this challenge. It might look simple, but hopping over The King's tie is going to get increasingly harder as it begins to spin faster and faster in time to the music.

Stay in the middle of the platform to give yourself a chance to regain your balance if the tie hits you, and collect those all-important score bubbles!

## Skateboard Freefall

This is an easy challenge to complete, but it takes a lot of practice to make the difference between finishing the level and finishing it well!

The most important thing to pull off is the start. Push the board and jump on it as fast as you can, then grab hold of the rough texture on the board's surface and pound the ✖ button whenever the wheels hit the ground to go faster. Don't sit too far forward on the board or you're likely to tip it over on some of the jumps.

## On to the Next Kingdom

If you thought The King's Gardens were a challenge, you haven't seen anything yet! The King is only one of eight Creator Curators and King Zola, the fearsome lion, is in charge of the baking-hot Savannah levels. The tutorial is over, so jump in that submarine and get ready to face stampeding buffalo and lost meerkats and to try and make amends for breaking Zola's precious statue as you continue your journey!

ZOLA

# The Savannah:
## Swinging Safari

ZOLA

You're not off to a great start with King Zola as your submarine smashes into his prized statue, so off you go to his castle to apologize. The Savannah is certainly a very spiky place, but luckily there are a herd of helpful giraffes willing to lift you up into the branches to continue your journey. The monkeys whose tails you grab onto while swinging through the treetops might not be as smooth to swing on as the sponges on strings from the previous levels, but their jittery movements can take you to secret areas, so keep your eyes peeled.

As you near Zola's palace, you will have to take care to dodge the baboons with the fiery bottoms, but once you confront the great lion he promises to forgive you for smashing his statue, as long as you find out what it is that has been bothering the buffalo so much. Dodging the early signs of a stampede, you make your way to the edge of the forest, where a helpful monkey tells you that he knows what has been disturbing the beasts.

## *Tricky Challenges*

Despite its wild appearance, the Savannah eases you into Zola's kingdom gently, and, despite the spikes, you can cross the dangerous jungle floor with ease to get to the end of the level. It's only when you head off in search of the many hidden items in the treetops that keeping your balance can become a challenge.

Other than that, watch out for the baboons. There is only a split second for you to avoid getting burned while passing under them. You can survive a brief scalding, so make sure to rest every time you're singed, because otherwise the burns will kill you!

## Favorite Items

If there is anybody out there in the world of LittleBigPlanet who *doesn't* like the giant **Zebra Head Object**, we have yet to meet them. Collect it at the beginning of the level, along with the various other jungle costume bits and pieces and, together with the **Zebra Costume** for the rest of your body, you'll soon be blending in with the wild animals that surround you.

Before you leave your submarine behind, stop and look around—if you enjoyed smashing into that statue, you'll be glad to find the **Submarine Launcher Object** among the wreckage!

**The Savannah**

There are loads of secret items in this level, so keep an eye on the top of the screen for items that might be a few hops up in the branches. Keep track of their position so that once you find a route up there, you can go back for them.

The most impressive stashes of secret items are at the **English Rose Sticker** switch near the beginning of the level (ignore the sign that tells you to turn left up the other giraffe's neck and keep going) and the **Horse Sticker** switch near the end of the level (turn left after leaving Zola, and the horse is beneath his throne).

If you really want to impress your friends, show them the solution to the **Horror Face Sticker** that appears to be boxed in on all sides by the landscape. Retrace your steps until you're beneath the giraffe, then hop backward to the rear plane behind the tree root. Now you can walk behind the landscape with ease to retrieve the item.

# The Savannah: Burning Forest

It's a forest fire! Leap on the backs of the stampeding buffalo to avoid a nasty death on the burning ground, and make your way up the mountain paths. But you're not out of danger yet, as the rampaging beasts are being swallowed by a giant crocodile! Swing across the zebra-patterned sponges to avoid the gaping jaws of these reptiles and make your way over the gaseous green swamps where they live. Soon you arrive at the entrance to a cave, shaped like the mouth of a crocodile, and sure enough you have to drop through chasms lined with the monsters. At the bottom of the caves are a series of strange creatures with bubbles for brains—pop them to discover a herd of meerkats attacking a poor crocodile. The Meerkat Mum thinks he has eaten her son—you need to clear his name!

## Tricky Challenges

If you manage to keep your balance on the buffalo long enough to reach the checkpoint at the top of the hill, don't bother jumping onto the platform to activate it. You'll be more likely to miss the jump back onto their hides as they roll down the hill. Concentrate on keeping your balance and timing that last-minute leap of faith to the nearest sponge to avoid being eaten!

The strange spiky monsters at the bottom of the cave may look fierce, but if you move to a plane in front of or behind them, they cannot harm you. A quick jump as they go past will burst their bubble brains regardless. Remember that jumping on these creatures will give your jump an extra boost, so use them to reach those object bubbles above them!

## Favorite Items

Tame the **Feathered Spikys** for use in your own level by boosting off one of them to grab the object above their heads!

There are some great items available as a reward for the two-player puzzle in this level. Find a friend and get them to hold the ramp down long enough for you to get up it and grab the **Tiger Nose Decoration** and **Antlers Costume Piece**.

## Secret Gifts

It might look tempting to jump off the buffalo at the nearest platform, but sometimes following the herd can take you to some interesting places. Stay on the stream of buffalo moving to the left until you reach an out-of-the-way area with a **Cat Head Sticker** switch to grab some goodies. (You'll need to have completed the next level to gain them, though!)

**The Savannah**

# The Savannah: Meerkat Kingdom

Descending deep into the Meerkat Mum's world, you get caught in a rockslide and slip into a labyrinth of prize bubbles and a quick race against time. As you progress further, you'll see the meerkats hiding in their burrows as you approach and discover caves full of wondrous score bubbles and items!

Eventually you discover the Meerkat Mum, who is complaining that her son, Stripy Tail, is out past his bedtime. You head to an underground club (a two-player paradise) and retrieve the errant child, who allows you to sneak past the bouncers for extra goodies.

Once Stripy is home safe, all that is left is for you to springboard off the meerkats' heads to safety!

## Tricky Challenges

There's nothing too tricky about the Meerkat Mum's lair, but if you want to get the highest score possible, it's worth planning your route through the various mazes you find along your way. It might not be obvious at first, but some paths don't allow you to backtrack, whereas others will let you access all areas.

When using the zebra-patterned levers to descend into the caves, look out for secret stashes of items that might be worth an early jump to grab!

The Meerkat Kingdom is great for playing with a friend, and together you can have fun jumping on the stomachs of the larger meerkats to catapult your buddy into the air and get those hard-to-reach items.

## Favorite Items

There are some pretty surreal
prizes available down here,
and you'll need a friend to get our favorites. First, use Stripy to get
the bouncer to let you into the little cubbyhole beneath the club so
that you can get the **Wooden Flamingo Object**. Then use a friend
to fire yourself onto the platform on the top right of the club for the
ultimate sticker— **Mr. Beaver Says No**!

## Secret Gifts

Whoa there! When you start the
level, don't go down. Turn right
instead, because hidden behind
the wall is a **Fluffy Tree Sticker**
switch (which you'll have if you
were the exploring type in Swinging Safari). Slap that on and the cave
will collapse, showering you with items!

Those cunning meerkats think they can buy you off with trinkets,
but we know better. Just above that circle of meerkats, after the
timer has finished, there is a pair in the top right corner pretending
to mind their own business. Swing over to them and they will retract
to reveal some crazy **Cow-Themed Stickers** just a short hop over
some spikes.

# The Savannah: Mini Levels

## Flaming Seesaws

The key to this mini level is in the Burning Forest level and is pretty tough to find unless you know where to look. Move along the back plane to jump over the monkey on the left of the entrance, and navigate a seesaw through the flames to find it.

Initially it seems like a fairly straightforward seesaw exercise. Move slowly to make sure the inclines are reversed completely before continuing and you should complete the level relatively easily. But hold on, there's more! A medium and hard version of the level are both unlocked and you must take care to pull some of the seesaws down, using their foam grip as you approach—this will save you time in the long run. Some of the seesaws have flames in the middle now, but remember, you can survive being scorched once.

The hard level has a helpfully placed pinball flipper to get you over the hardest parts of the level toward the end, so watch out for it!

## Tunnel Plunge

The key to this mini level is found toward the end of the Meerkat Kingdom level, and if you take care to bounce on all the meerkat heads you should find yourself thrown into it without any trouble.

Race through a twisty cavern and avoid the spikes. Sound hard? It's not really. Let yourself go with the flow of the rotating wheels and rock falls and you should find yourself missing the traps automatically. At the bottom of one particularly long series of cogs, there is a tricky spiked pit beneath you, but a quick jump will save your life, and if not, at least you'll be ready for it the second time!

## Meerkat Bounce

If you used Stripy's VIP credentials to get the bouncers to let you into their exclusive areas, this key should be pretty easy to find. Bounce along a row of meerkat heads, grabbing score bubbles and avoiding the flaming logs. It's easy at first, but soon the level will start to throw some nasty surprises your way. If you live long enough to get to the stage where the fiery lizard heads begin to snap at you, get past them by jumping underneath while their mouths are closed.

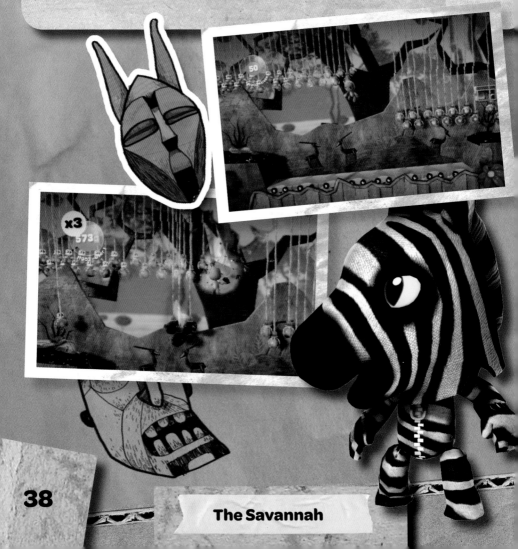

**The Savannah**

**Sardinalla PESCADO**

**FRIDA**

## On to the Next Kingdom

Thanks to your success in the Meerkat Kingdom, you are invited to try and save Frida and Don Lu's wedding. You travel to a dark kingdom filled with skeletons, monsters, and mad scientists to find out what is making the jilted bride so angry, and preventing Frida and her lover from living happily ever after . . .

# FRIDA

# The Wedding:
# The Wedding Reception

You arrive at the reception to find that Frida's groom has gone missing and, stopping only to pick up the appropriate attire, set off to explore this gothic kingdom in search of the absent Don Lu.

Moving past wobbly pillars, buoyant balloons, and elastic sponges, you finally have to cross a treacherous swamp by jumping through the mouths of skeletons. A few quick bounces on some springy platforms take you to Frida, only to discover that Don Lu has descended to the crypts!

## *Tricky Challenges*

If you want the **Wooden Sword** item of clothing for completing the level with no lives lost, you're going to have to be very careful at the Wedding Reception. Some skeletal mouths won't open until you have already jumped across to them, so time your leaps of faith carefully.

The most difficult obstacles to navigate, though, are the spring platforms. Make sure to do big jumps rather than just tapping the ✖ button, and only do so while the platform is moving up. A few of these and you'll be soaring into the clouds and discovering a few goodies along the way!

## Favorite Items

How can any Sack Person not look adorable in the **Veil** or **Bow Tie** that you receive at the beginning of this level? Although running about with that sheet trailing behind you can be rather impractical. Now also seems a good time to point out that if you change the speech bubble color schemes in the Popit menu, your clothes will color coordinate to match!

If you want to play the Wedding Reception's foot-tapping tune in your own level, simply complete the sticker switch by filling in the skeleton's missing eye (you can find the eye sticker in that tiny arena with the elastic foam ball and the button springboard) to get the **Volver a Comenzar Audio**.

And finally, don't forget the easy sticker switch right at the beginning of the level. Grab the **Skeleton Hat Sticker** from the balloon area and backtrack (or most likely replay the level) to the platform above the first roving butler. Slap it on to receive some easy prizes.

**The Wedding**

## Secret Gifts

If you're still feeling brave after navigating the opening mouths of the skeletons over that pit of purple fog, try using the springboard mouth at the end to get on top of their heads, and retrace your steps along the top to pick up some goodies.

Remember those two springboard skeleton heads right at the end of the level? Use the second one to bounce to the left, and time your jump so you land on the Waving Skeleton's hat! The camera angle hid these prize bubbles from you as you were passing beneath him earlier, but there's also a challenge key up there as well!

# The Wedding:
# The Darkness

The crypts are dark and dangerous, but luckily you have Don Lu's dog to guide you. Ride on his back to reach those hard-to-get items and help clear a path for him so he can guide you deeper into the level.

But what's this? A trapdoor swallows the dog and he is taken away by an evil man known as the Collector. Now you have to go it alone, but luckily the candles will light your way as long as you move slowly enough. A few skeletal lifts (bristling with spiky teeth) later and you stumble across Don Lu! Too exhausted to continue, take him as far as you can. When he's safe, you can continue without him, only to find that Frida has gone on a rampage in her skulldozer! Use the wreckage to reach the end of the level, and continue on to confront the machine!

## Tricky Challenges

Be sure to take your time in the Darkness—the light will only illuminate a short distance in front of you, and leaping into the dark is a sure-fire way to a spiky end.

Don Lu's dog might be helpful, but he can get you into trouble. Take the lower path while he travels through the gaseous cave, and be sure to jump the moment he touches the trapdoor to avoid suffering the same fate as him!

The skull lifts can be a pain, but the easiest way to navigate them is not to jump—simply walk from platform to platform to avoid their sharp teeth.

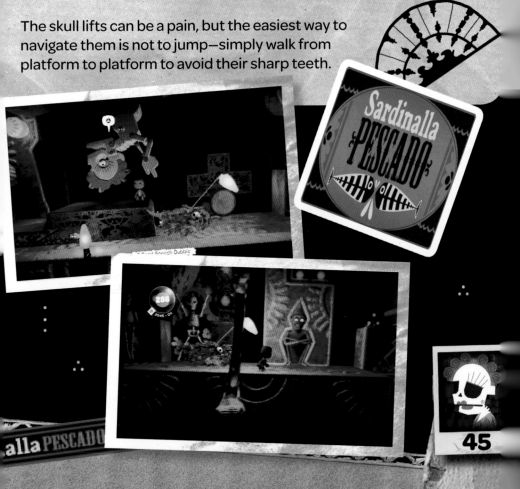

## Favorite Items

For the Sackgirls out there, complete the level for a funky **Pink Dot Costume** and **Fairy Wings**, and for the Sackboys, you'll need to be a careful spelunker, because you need to complete the level without dying to receive the **Roman Armor Costume**.

A not-so-well-hidden sticker switch will also give you the rather funky **Bunny** and **Brown Leather Costumes**. On the last set of skull lifts, jump left instead of right to find a sticker switch requiring six copies of the **Pixel Skull Sticker**, which you should already have.

**The Wedding**

## Secret Gifts

Apart from the multitude of two-player puzzles out there, you can find a couple of secret treats. The easiest to spot are those that appear to be buried in the walls of the cave on the side of a skull lift. There is a secret passage halfway up on both occasions, so just keep walking right to get inside.

Also, try moving to the farthest back plane while walking past the candlelit sections—there are usually some items hidden behind the pillars.

The most difficult secret item, though, is at the top of the first set of skull lifts immediately after the trapdoor. Use the momentum of the final lift to jump up and out onto the top of the final skull to get the **Picture Frame Object**. Then, repeat the process, but this time jump to the left to grab the swinging skull for a challenge key and **The Appliance of Science** Audio.

# The Wedding: Skulldozer

Frida's skulldozer rampage continues and this time you are right in the way of her giant mechanical beasty! Run as fast as you can and hop across platforms to avoid the approaching pits of lava as her machine knocks over everything in its path. Get too close and the skulldozer will pour burning logs out of its mouth at you, and be careful to stay on the right plane to avoid being trapped in the wreckage of the platforms.

Luckily, the mechanical monster is too heavy for the bridge and falls to its doom, only for Frida to discover that Don Lu hadn't stood her up after all. What a crazy misunderstanding!

## Tricky Challenges

The checkpoint gate follows you as you make your way through the level, and this time around you have a lot of lives to spare, so it's likely that you will be able to complete this level the first time around. If you want to collect all the items, you'll no doubt miss a few when you're spawned further along with each death. The tricky part is completing Skulldozer without dying—it might look easier just to run along the floor on the front plane, but jumping on the platforms can help you get over those extra-wide lava pits.

## Favorite Items

It might take you a couple of run-throughs, but if you manage to collect all the items on this level you get your own **Skulldozer Object** as a reward! Don't worry about jumping on all the platforms to grab the various items along the way, as most of the time they will be thrown to an easier-to-reach spot as the skulldozer smashes into them:

To get the music for this level you'll need to jump onto the final wedding guest before the bridge—or simply grab her to topple her over!

## Secret Gifts

Complete your **Roman Costume** by finishing this level without dying to get a fancy **Roman Helmet** to go with your **Wooden Sword** and **Roman Armor** from the previous two levels. Other than that, there are no secret items on this level, and the only difficulty will be in staying alive long enough to grab everything else!

# The Wedding: Mini Levels

## Wobble Poles

The challenge key for Wobble Poles is located in the Wedding Reception. If you can synchronize your jumps with the last spring platform, you should be able to jump high enough to reach it with ease.

Race against time to collect as many points as you can before you reach the end of the level. Try and stay on the platforms for as long as possible, but don't worry if you fall to the ground— it's still possible to complete the level. Be careful of the large spread of spikes beneath the springy platforms toward the end— you'll need to jump as far as possible to grab the sponges, which will save you from returning to the previous checkpoint.

## The Dangerous Descent

The challenge key for the Dangerous Descent is on top of the giant waving skeleton's hat. Use the bouncing skulls that are immediately after it to get to the ledge near his head and jump as he tilts toward you.

The rules for this game are simple: Don't touch the top or bottom of the screen. The Descent starts off easy enough, but be careful of those drops that are two or three levels deep, as they can easily plunge you too far down. Try and zigzag from level to level to stay in control.

## Bubble Labyrinth

Collect the challenge key for the Labyrinth by boosting your jump to the left while going up the third skull on the first set of lifts. Grab hold of the skull on the rope and swing across to the left-hand platform for the key.

Beat the timer by pushing the foam blocks out of the way to find the quickest route out of the cave. Be careful of running into the fiery coals that can block your path—the safest and quickest route is along the top two levels of the maze. But remember that collecting score bubbles will pause the timer, so experiment with different routes until you find the perfect balance of score bubbles and speed!

**The Wedding**

## JALAPENO

### On to the Next Kingdom

With Frida and Don finally happy in each other's arms, join them on their honeymoon in Jalapeno's Canyons—home of Jalapeno, the master of explosives. If you think that sounds like a less-than-relaxing place to vacation, then you'd be right, so prepare to dodge mine carts and timed explosives as you attempt to break Don's uncle out of jail!

**JALAPENO**

# The Canyons:
# Boom Town

The honeymooners might be happy, but no one else in Boom Town is. Poor old Jalapeno is locked in jail by the evil Sheriff Zapata for all the trouble he's been causing, leaving it up to you to break him out while dodging the leftover explosives and jumping a canyon on a rocket along the way.

The Collector pops up again while you're doing this, snatching Frida and Don Lu away from their honeymoon retreat, but there's no time to worry about that, as no sooner is Jalapeno free than you're sent tumbling down a mine shaft for a lesson in explosives. Finally, you break through into the mines and ride a handy cart to safety.

## Tricky Challenges

The opening of this level is one of the toughest, so don't stop moving while navigating those cacti or else the wobbly rock piles will give way beneath you!

Watch out for any piles of explosives and make sure to move to a safe distance away before detonating. Take a moment to wait for any flaming debris that might be rolling your way afterward as well, just in case.

The hardest challenge in the entire level is carrying those impact bombs around on your jetpack; go too fast and they could swing you out of control and into the nearest moving stalactite! Very annoying if you're trying to finish the level with no lives lost.

**Wrestling Mask!** Put it on the moment you receive it at the beginning of the level and don't take it off until we tell you . . . which is never!

Hey, you know what would go well with that wrestling mask you have on? How about some **Cowboy Boots**? Complete the level without losing a life to win this fancy footwear.

For other general goodness, be sure to check behind the cacti and in the blown-up prison for some more of the sweet stuff. And while you're carrying that explosive truck through the scorpions, quickly jump on its back to grab those three objects in the alcove.

## Secret Gifts

Piñata time now—see that cat hanging around innocently when you first enter the town? Jump up and grab it. A few good swings and it will split open, showering you with all manner of gifts.

You might be in a rush to break Jalapeno out of jail, but you can wait long enough to perform a dangerous sticker puzzle. When you first pass through the scorpions to get to the explosive cart, leave it where it is and drag the big foam block across so that you can jump up and over the ridge on the right. In a small cave you'll find an Orange Bird shooting gallery—hit them all for some stickers as well as the **Cornman** Audio. Be careful not to miss, though—each time you do, some bombs will drop from above.

57

# The Canyons:
# The Mines

The Sheriff is hiding out in the mines and Jalapeno sends you in after him. Dodging Aztec Spikys and clinging onto huge felt balls, you hitch a lift in a mine cart into the bowels of the complex. An encounter with some jumping clowns, the mine's lift system, a race against time, and yet more giant rotating felt balls later and you're finally pursued down the last stretch by a huge ball of fire, only to discover that Sheriff Zapata has fled into the Serpent Shrine!

## Tricky Challenges

Remember to unload the buckets before jumping in them to get across the chasm near the beginning of the level. And while you're making your way across the rotating felt balls, cling on for dear life to find some extra items around the other side. Be careful: Some of those wheels don't have any grip and sometimes a section of them is embedded in the flames—so make sure you're ready to hop off at any minute!

When you start the timed section, make sure you give yourself room to stand far enough back before the timed explosives detonate. Two explosives at a time should make a hefty dent in that wall without making things too dangerous for you while you're pushing them down the slope!

While being pursued by that great ball of fire, use little jumps to cross the hot coals. Anything longer and you'll find yourself sailing onto the next piece of burning ground rather than safe rock.

The **Mine-Cart Object** is great for your own levels—grab it while swinging from the green foam ball that links one cart route to another.

Ever want to dress your Sack Person up as a hillbilly? Now's your chance, with the two-player section situated at the end of the last truck route. Follow those three score bubbles up the ramp into a secret area to confront another diabolical wheel challenge and receive **Dungarees** and **Rotten Teeth**!

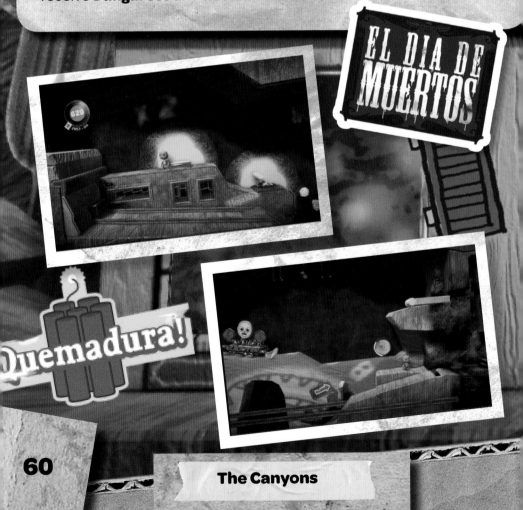

## Secret Gifts

There are a few sticker switches lying off the beaten track (including a **Wrestler Sticker** one, which you'll find the sticker for in the following level). These can be found to the right of the second giant wheel, on the left-hand side of the upper bucket puzzle, and up near the two-player section at the end of the final mine-cart route. But by far the most interesting secret rewards on this level come from the imaginative use of explosives!

Instead of pushing those timed explosives down the slope in the race section, pull one of them back to the cardboard panel. The blast will tear it open to reveal your own **Timed Explosive Object**, among other things.

The second explosive-themed puzzle is toward the end of the race section. Instead of heading left toward the finishing posts, head over to the cart whose front end is an explosive box and whose rear is a detonation button. Don't blow it up just yet—instead, push it over to the right and then jump on the button to cause a rockslide filled with items.

Last of all, there's a parting gift right at the end of the level. Speak to Jalapeno, then retrace your steps, but this time go up the rock slope on your left to find a **Green Gecko Sticker**.

# The Canyons:
# Serpent Shrine

The Serpent Shrine is a winding labyrinth filled with snakes, and you'll have to be quick on your toes to avoid these beasties. Use the foam balls that quickly retract to keep you out of the path of the larger beasts and avoid the rock falls that will cave in from the roof. Once you've managed to make it through this area, though, the worst is yet to come, as you battle Sheriff Zapata in an epic final showdown.

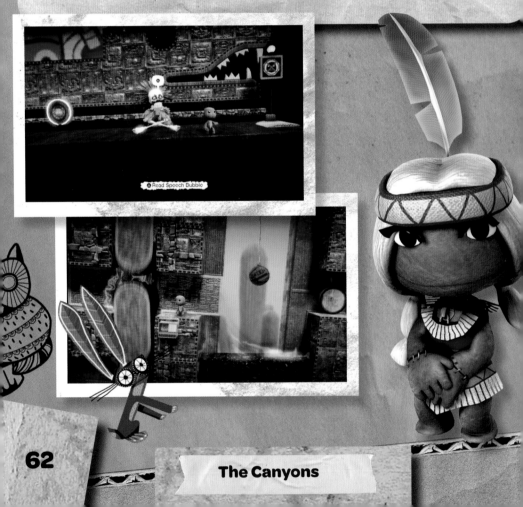

## Tricky Challenges

It is easy to get lost in this level, and if you find yourself stuck, try backtracking to see if you missed another route. It's inevitable that you'll have to sometimes take a short journey down the paths of some of the larger snakes, but there's always an alcove to take cover in if your time runs out.

The smaller three bubble snakes can be a pain to defeat, but it's worth doing as they almost always hide an item or object.

The Sheriff is a tough baddie to dispose of, so learn his moves. In the first round he'll throw impact bombs at long, medium, and short range, followed by a timed explosive. Dodge these while dragging the timed explosives to break through the wall (three should do it) and get him backed up against his dynamite store.

Once there, you'll need to do the same again, but this time across a series of moving platforms. He'll throw a timed explosive to the farthest-left platform and the easiest way to get it over to him is through the middle of the center platform, then over the top of the right-hand one. You only need two successful explosions to send the Sheriff packing!

# Hojaldra

## Favorite Items

If you've been running around the Canyons with that wooden sword you received in Boom Town (for completing the level without dying), now's the time for an upgrade. Simply complete the level to receive a hefty **Frying Pan**—now you're cooking!

At the top of the second long, patterned sponge lift and to the right is the **Mexican Wrestler Sticker** needed to complete the sticker switch from the previous level!

## Secret Gifts

There are three secret sticker switches in this level. The first uses the **Aztec Face Sticker** and is in a small alcove past the second fire pit, near the beginning of the level.

The second is after a series of launching pads and uses the **Green Gecko Sticker** that was hidden at the end of the previous level. Use this to unlock the awesome **Clown Costume**, among other things.

Above the rickety bridge that collapses when you cross it is the third sticker switch. You'll need to retrace your steps and go up a few levels to find the block that you need to push out of the way to gain access to a secret passage. This will take you out into the open and along a red beam to a golden snake mouth. Use the **Orange Motif Sticker** you collected from the previous sticker switch to activate it.

# The Canyons: Mini Levels

## Wrestler's Drag

The challenge key for this level is in the cat piñata before the bank in Boom Town; break it open to grab it.

Drag Luchador to his match before the time runs out! There are no score bubbles in this mini level so save time by hammering the ❌ button to add power to your pushes and throw him down the steeper slopes so that you can catch up with him at the bottom. Be careful, though; Luchador is so big he could easily squash you between a rock and a hard place if you don't watch out.

## Cowabunga

Grab the key from the cow at the beginning of Boom Town—you can't miss it!

Ride the cow for as long as possible without falling in the gassy swamp beneath. This challenge starts off easy, as the cow sways from side to side, but soon it will buck so steeply that you will have to jump to avoid slipping from its back—timing is everything!

## Roller Run

Unsurprisingly, considering how much this level features fabric wheels, this key is in one of the bigger fabric wheel sections of the Mines and should be easy to spot.

Beat the timer and avoid getting burned by grabbing hold of the fabric wheels and making your way across the flaming pit. It's not easy and you'll be tearing your hair out when you realize that there are medium and hard levels to be unlocked once you complete the first. Don't try and grab onto all the wheels—a quick run and jump across the top will do. Watch out for the wheels with no grip— there are usually sponge wheels nearby that allow you to circumvent them. Finally, take care when releasing from the faster-moving wheels to avoid overshooting your target.

## Puzzle Wheel

A simple puzzle now—collect the challenge key from the mines as it dangles halfway along one of your fiery mine-cart journeys.

For this level, you need to get three jade stones into the bottom right-hand corner to unlock the way out. Pull the lever right until all the jade stones are together, then nudge it back and forth to try and give them enough momentum to all topple out of the exit together.

MAGS

## On to the Next Kingdom

After all this excitement it's Jalapeno's turn to want a break, and he invites you to the Metropolis to meet Mags the Mechanic. Prepare to battle through scrapyards and along the top of subway cars to continue your adventure through this bustling urban sprawl as you prepare to compete in a race against Mags's nemesis, Ze Dude.

**MAGS**

# The Metropolis: Lowrider

Approaching the city in Uncle Jalapeno's old banger, you are immediately told by Mags to get some new wheels. Easier said than done, as you work your way through the scrapyard, bouncing on the hoods of lowriders and dodging the electrocuting rollers. A few switch-pulls later and you're rewarded with a brand-new car. Mags thinks that it is so fast you could take on Ze Dude in a race. This evil man has stolen Mags's own car and as you race through the Metropolis he crashes it into the subway. I guess you'll just have to go down and get it back . . .

## Tricky Challenges

Driving the lowriders might be fun, but they're a bit tricky to get the hang of. Beware of sharp bumps, which can throw you to the other end of the driver's seat and start you driving in the wrong direction!

Most of the level is pretty straightforward, but beware the spinning bicycle wheels section—the lower one has a couple of shocking surprises to dodge as it revolves. If you feel like exploring to grab all the items in this level, be prepared to hop through a few tight spots. Remember, synchronize your jumps with the lowrider hoods to get that extra height boost.

## Favorite Items

What could sum up the city more than a prehistoric dinosaur tail? No? Well, get one anyway by completing the level without dying!

If dinosaurs aren't to your liking, bling it up with a dollar chain, mirror shades, and a tracksuit—then color coordinate using the player color option in the Popit.

## Secret Gifts

There are a few tricky routes for extra goodies, but they're well worth attempting! First of all, replay the level once you've grabbed the **Route 77 Sticker** and slap it on the signpost at the beginning of the level for the **Fruity Logo** and **Dripping Smile Stickers**. Don't forget about that logo, though, because when Mags rewards you with your new car at the end of Lowrider, you can stick it on the side for some car part objects.

For another sticker puzzle, use the second hopping hot rod just after you meet Mags to propel you into the small booth on the right with the hard-to-see lever—this will open up another area with two taxi cabs. Use the **Pink Blaster Sticker** to get them hopping about so that you can reach some goodies.

Finally, let's get that **Statue of Liberty Sticker** you've been eyeing up above the new costume area. Jump left on the third hot rod hood at the beginning and grab onto the lamps above. Swing through the electrocuted rollers and drop down when you reach the building. There is a hole in the wall there that will let you grab hold of a streetlight to get to the top of the costume building. Repeat the process again, but this time go to the left for even more prizes.

# The Metropolis: Subway

Travel down into the dark depths of the sewers and hop on the subway trains to avoid the deadly electrified rails. Along the way, you'll need to dodge all sorts of obstacles to stay on the back of these metal monsters before getting lost in the ventilation system. Once you've recovered, though, Mags has arrived with her grabber to help you get her car out of the swamp. Mission completed, you take the elevator back to the surface only to see the Collector running off with Ze Dude—this doesn't look good.

## Tricky Challenges

There are a lot of prize bubbles in this level, but you'll need to play through it a few times to get them all, especially on the elevator down. Try asking a buddy to come along for the ride to help you.

Staying on the back of the trains can be a pain, but a few well-timed jumps should see you on your way. Be careful to stay near the front of the cars to give yourself some space if you miss a jump and, if you find yourself too far back, get off and wait for the next one.

The ventilation system can take you in directions you really don't want to go, so to get that challenge key you'll have to be very careful not to descend too far, too early.

DONUTS

## Favorite Items

With that dinosaur tail and scaly skin outfit, grab the **Glove Puppet** to match by finishing the level without losing a life.

After helping Mags get her car out of the swamp, don't run off too quickly—in the trunk of the car is the **Mags's Car Object** to use in your own levels.

They might not protect you from the electric railway lines, but they'll certainly keep the sewer water out. Simply complete the level to earn a pair of **Wellington Boots**.

COFFEE

CHUG lite

## Secret Gifts

Two sticker switches here, and both can be easily missed—so keep your eyes peeled!

When you first get off the elevator, and before jumping on the nearest train, look at the gap between the carriages. There's an outline for the **Fries Sticker** you have in your collection. Stick it on before the next train to get the **White Weave Costume** and **Subway Train Object**.

Use the **Intense Blue Graffiti Sticker**, which you'll pick up in the next level, to tag the wall just before the timed section for some stickers and the **Shiny Metal** material.

# The Metropolis:
# The Construction Site

Poor old Mags; today really isn't going her way and now Ze Dude and his goons are trashing her construction site! Dodge the rolling balls of fire and jump from wobbly beam to wobbly beam as you climb higher and higher into the scaffolding for a final epic confrontation between Ze Dude, his bouncers, and their flame guns!

## Tricky Challenges

The flaming balls might look dangerous, but actually you can dodge most of them by moving into the back plane as they roll past—simple.

More difficult, however, are the wobbly girders. You'll need to set them rocking to be able to move upward to the next platforms, so be careful not to tip yourself down into the red gas. Either run from end to end or jump up and down on them until they're rocking high enough for you to run and jump across.

Ze Dude's guard dogs might look frightening, but you can use them to your advantage. Hopping on their bubble brains will give your jump a boost and help you get to those hard-to-reach items.

Ze Dude himself is a far deadlier opponent. Use the platform to bounce the balls of fire back up at him. Hit him and his bouncers on the red switch to blow them up!

## Favorite Items

If you manage to dodge all of those fire balls, balance on the beams, and defeat Ze Dude without losing any lives, you can complete your level-acing outfit with a **Dinosaur Mask Object**. Also, don't forget to grab Ze Dude's private jet prize bubble from under his plane before going up the steps.

For those of an artistic persuasion, go to the two-player section just up and after you dodge the rolling basketball–head monster. Turn left and solve the two-player puzzle with a friend to get the stylish **Red Stiletto Object**, among other things.

## Secret Gifts

This level is very hard to navigate, so exploring might be the last thing on your mind, but it's well worth your while. Remember the elevator with the mermaid on it? When you bring it up to the second platform, rock it back and forth to get yourself up to reach the third level on the right. If you run along the beam you'll encounter an epic sticker puzzle. Use your **Cityscape Stickers** to fill in all six blanks and a larger beam will descend with tons of prize bubbles for you to collect.

Ze Dude's third guard dog comes in handy for this puzzle. Use its bubble brain to leap onto the retractable sponge above its head and raise yourself up to the highest point on the level. Here are three wobbly girders with a few prize bubbles balanced on the ends, and at the very top is an elusive challenge key. It might take a while to rock the girders enough to get it, but it's worth the effort.

# The Metropolis:
# Mini Levels

## The Drag Race

Find the challenge key for the Drag Race right above your second hot rod, and use the bouncing hood to jump up and grab it.

Grab the sponge in whichever car you choose to accelerate and reach the finish line before your opponent. Be careful of the boxes at the end, though; they can bring you to a swift halt just before the finish.

## Elevation

If you managed to reach the challenge key in the ventilation system on the Subway level, you can now put your reflexes and judgment to the test as you race against time in not one, but three elevators, to collect as many score bubbles as you can before the timer runs out. All the while, you'll be dodging the deadly gas vents. It's worth taking the risk on this level as each score bubble you collect pauses the timer and boosts your final score!

440

## The Discombobulator

Collect the challenge key from on top of the highest scaffolding to play the Discombobulator—a surreal game where you have to jump over fast food as it runs along a conveyer belt beneath your feet, as well as dodge hot coals to collect score bubbles. You can grab the food, so try pushing it onto the coals to protect yourself from the longer jumps, and be careful to avoid the edges of the screen as the belt begins to move faster and faster.

**The Metropolis**

**SENSEI**

## On to the Next Kingdom

Impressed with the way you defeated him and his bouncers so quickly, Ze Dude offers to let you borrow his plane and take off to the Islands, so that you can refine your skills at the hands of Grandmaster Sensei. This Eastern land might look like a paradise, but you'll need to do a bit of tidying up before you can stop and enjoy the scenery . . .

# The Islands: Endurance Dojo

The moment you arrive on the island, Grandmaster Sensei wants you to help her battle the Terrible Oni—but first she needs to see if you have what it takes. This level is designed to test your skills as a ninja, and you'll need them as you run across special bridges made of planks, jump from fans to pivoting foam wheels, and battle . . . er . . . sushi monsters.

## Tricky Challenges

------------------------------------

You need to be quick on your feet here—don't stop moving as you run across the ninja bridges or the wobbly fans as they will throw you off the moment you slow down. It's also good to get some momentum before jumping onto the pivoting foam wheels. That extra boost will help you get the hard-to-reach items above the first few checkpoints. The timed challenge toward the end of the level isn't required, but it will take a couple of tries to be able to do it in one try.

Welcome. I am Grandmaster Sensei. I shall hone your warrior skills in preparation for your encounter with The Terrible Oni.
◉ Close

## Favorite Items

Everybody loves ninjas, so follow the trend by dressing your Sackperson up as one! Collect the **Ninja Skin** and **Ninja Scarf** from the costume building at the beginning of the level.

If you don't like following the trend, complete the level to get the rather stylish **Escaped Convict Costume,** to show everyone what a bad boy your Sackperson is instead.

**The Islands**

## Secret Gifts

Just before you get to the large set of wheels that take you down to the end of the level, retrace your steps to the right once more, but this time go along the little platforms above the rickety bridge. This will take you to a sticker switch with some elegant rewards, as well as a challenge key.

Try the same trick again, but this time halfway through the level. Just before the trio of sushi monsters, go back along those little platforms and swing over the Sensei's head to find a series of tiny pillars with prize bubbles along the top. Don't worry too much if you fall, though, as there are some more goodies halfway down—just hope you land on one of the spinning platforms!

# The Islands:
# Sensei's Lost Castle

Timing is everything as you break into Sensei's castle to rescue her flame-throwing cat from the evil Sumo and his ninja minions. You'll have to hurl yourself over the wall on a giant catapult, then avoid assassins as they sneak up on you from behind the paper walls, then navigate a series of fiendish rotating balls before pausing for a quick balloon ride and the final ascent. At the top of the building, you'll have to get past the giant Sumo before you can release the cat and swing home to safety.

Planning to break into the castle? To get over the castle wall, try using the catapult. There should be some way to reposition it. And beware the evil Sumo!

● Close

## Tricky Challenges

The hardest obstacles in the castle are the spinning wheels—timing when you release from the previous one to jump to the next is crucial, and can mean the difference between life and death in the fiery basement below. Use the wheel's upward motion to boost your jumps to get the hard-to-reach items near the top of both wheel sections.

## Favorite Items

Getting the second challenge key in this level is a nightmare, but you can do it if you time your release from the last large green ball right. Use the momentum to boost your jump and land on top of the smaller swinging fabric ball. From there, you can grab the key with ease, as well as the rather funky *Song 2* **Audio**.

With all the peril you'll be facing in this level, it's a tough task to finish it without dying, but if you manage such a spectacular feat, you'll be rewarded with the hilarious **Googly Eye Glasses Costume** item—if that's not an incentive, we don't know what is!

**The Islands**

## Secret Gifts

It'll probably take a few goes, but if you bring the catapult close enough to the wall you can fling yourself into the crook of the house and pick up the **Japanese Wave Sticker**, as well as the **Catapult Object**. The wave sticker is particularly useful, as there is a secret sticker switch to the left-hand side of the floor just above the first green wheel; fill in the wall painting for a treasure trove of rewards.

To get the **Thin Ninja Object** that appears to be buried in the wall, just before you get to the sumo bodyguards, you'll need to drag the fabric ball from the two-player puzzle back along the corridor. Drag it to the tiny magnetic switch by the wall and the case will open to release your item.

# The Islands: The Terrible Oni's Volcano

Time for a breather now as you take the flying machine through the Islands' night sky before stopping off to pick up supplies in two buildings on your way to the Terrible Oni's volcano. Descending through the mouth of the mountain, you dodge past flaming rock flows and cross huge lava pits until you confront the deadly enemy. Luckily, the Sensei's flame-throwing cat is there to help you and, working together, you blast Oni into a thousand bits.

Use my flying machine to get to The Terrible Oni's Volcano. Grab the sponges to go up, right and left.
● Close

## Tricky Challenges

You'll need to become a master of the flying machine controls to be able to collect all the items that dot the night sky. Remember that even though the left and right sponges are for steering, they'll still propel you upward, so use them while descending for any delicate maneuvering.

The boss fight with the Terrible Oni is actually fairly simple compared to what has come before—jump up the little steps to the back row while being careful to dodge the sword, and once there, you are safe from Oni's cutlass, which will drop harmlessly in front of you. Run over to the switch that will move the flame-throwing cat toward your enemy, moving quickly to the right to dodge the flaming balls that Oni will spew in your direction at regular intervals. Repeat this three or four times to get the cat close enough to destroy the monster!

## Favorite Items

If you had fun with the flying machine, you'll be pleased to discover that the object is given to you as a reward for completing the level, so be prepared to build some tall towers for the machine to circumvent in your own levels.

Be sure to collect all the items as you go down the mouth of the volcano because one of them is the **Japanese Stork Sticker**, which you can use at the end of the Endurance Dojo to unlock even more prize bubbles.

## Secret Gifts

Explore the sky just to the right of the first tower to discover a missing cloud. The **Bouncy Cloud Sticker** is actually later in the level, in front of a Sensei and next to the side of the volcano. Once you've picked it up, go back and fill in the gap for the **Fairy Star Wand Costume** and the **Wind Charm Decoration**.

There is another sticker switch in the second tower—just to the left and above that stairway of spikes is a hard-to-spot room. Go inside and use the **Sakura Flower Sticker** to gain the **Rainbow Tree Object** and **Pretty Leaf Sticker**.

# The Islands: Mini Levels

## Daruma San

The key for this level is toward the end of the Endurance Dojo. Backtrack over the small platforms just before the final fabric ball descent to find a little platform with a sticker switch and the challenge key.

This level might look easy, but you'll have to keep your balance to complete it within the time limit. The round blocks will wobble and tumble beneath you, so keep moving if you don't want to spend time pushing blocks together to get you back on track.

## Wheel of Misfortune

The challenge key for the wheel of misfortune is in easy view above the rotating green fabric ball, just after the balloon section. You'll need to use the bounciness of the wheel to get that extra height to reach it, though.

Run along a three-leveled wheel, avoiding obstacles and getting score bubbles for as long as possible, as it gets faster and faster. The trick to remember here is that jumping will automatically take you up a level, so use it for quick dodges. It takes longer to jump down a level, so try and stay on the bottom level for as long as possible. Your running speed might be slowed by the movement of the wheel, but your jumps aren't, so use a quick burst of leaps and bounds to regain any lost ground quickly.

## Roller Castle

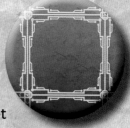

You have to jump on top of the smaller hanging fabric ball, just after reaching the top of the flaming fabric ball section and just before the final sumo showdown. It takes timing and practice to get on top of the ball and reach the key, so take care.

Grab the rollers to fling yourself up the castle, collecting score bubbles as you make your way to the top and the finish line. You shouldn't need to use any button other than **[R1]** once you get started, so concentrate on your timing and angles over everything else to reach the top in record time!

**MAGICIAN**

## On to the Next Kingdom

After your spectacular showdown with Oni, Grandmaster Sensei directs you to the Temples to buy a flame-throwing cat of your own! Take the flying machine and prepare to ride magic carpets, giant elephants, and undulating floors, and meet a mysterious magician as you battle through the magical, beautiful, and dangerous abodes of some strange and wondrous creatures.

**MAGICIAN**

# The Temples:
# The Dancer's Court

The shopkeeper is happy to supply you with a **Flame-Throwing Cat Object**, if you can reach it, and that goes the same for most of the items in the Dancer's Court. Spring off the waving arms of her worshippers, and leap from magic carpet to magic carpet before running along the back of a giant writhing snake. Finally,

take a rollercoaster ride down the undulating waves of the dancing floor to meet with the Goddess. She wants you to journey to the Great Magician's Temple to help him bring sharing back to LittleBigPlanet. Could this have something to do with the Collector we saw kidnapping yet more people halfway through this level?

## *Tricky Challenges*

- - - - - - - - - - - - - - - - - - - - - - - - - - - - - - - - - - - - -

Be careful on the magic carpets that are attached to rotating wheels: They are pivoted and will rock back and forth if you're not steady on your feet.

The motto for this level is simply to keep moving. Most obstacles might look impassable if you stop and think, but actually running straight into danger is often the easiest way through. Just make sure you don't stop!

The timed section on the golden platforms is probably the hardest section, and it should take you three different platforms to make it through alive and still get all the points. Don't give up hope if you get singed, though, as it's only on the second scalding that you'll be sent back to a checkpoint!

Dress the part in the **Turban** and **Sari Objects** that you receive at the beginning of the level, although whether these will go with the **Green Goggles** you get for finishing the level or the **Chicken Beak** for finishing it without dying is anybody's guess.

Also, what could be more useless than a giant **Rubber Snake Object**? Grab one at the feet of the Goddess, just to put it in people's ways during the creation mode . . .

**The Temples**

## Secret Gifts

There is a cheeky sticker switch at the beginning of the level that requires the **Prince Face Sticker** from later in the level. Replay the Dancer's Court once you've grabbed it to gain the **Ornate Column** and **Cardboard Arch Objects**.

You might be too busy dodging fire pits and platforming across magic carpets to notice this second sticker puzzle, but at the top of the very last magic carpet descent there is the outline of the Taj Mahal. Fill it in with the temple and tower stickers you've collected along the way to receive the **Girl Face**, **Girl Body**, and **Girl Arm Stickers**.

# The Temples:
# Elephant Temple

You begin your journey to the Great Magician's Palace, but the Swami warns you that to get there you must first pass through the Elephant Temple. There are many traps and switches in this level as you spring from moving platform to moving platform in an attempt to keep away from the deadly fire pits that litter the Temple. Switches must be pulled to create and extend pathways, and you will need to time your jumps well to avoid the rippling blocks that will attempt to crush you along the way. Finally, a great elephant will arrive to transport you for the final stretch, although you'll need to perform some swift acrobatics to avoid being thrown to the fiery coals beneath.

## Tricky Challenges

Timing is everything once again and deceptively simple paths have a habit of springing up as you approach, so be careful not to rush or you could find yourself running into a pillar of fire. Near the beginning of the level you will be catapulted up through a rippling set of platforms. Jump to the next level only when the platforms begin to move—leap too early and you will be crushed!

There are many occasions when you have to navigate two large, square blocks that shift around each other. It might look hard, but a quick run across the tops as they pass will get you through easily, although in doing so you might miss out on some items hidden in the walls.

## Favorite Items

Who wants to go swimming? Simply complete the level for the snazzy **Life Ring Costume**—it might not help you float over those dangerous fire pits, but it sure looks funny.

It was fun riding that **Mechanical Elephant Object**, wasn't it? Just after the elephant passes under the gate you open for it, jump backward off its back into the stone alcove to grab the prize bubble and use the creature in your own levels.

**The Temples**

## Secret Gifts

This level is all about the sticker switches, so make sure to go back and complete the **Blue Elephant** puzzle near the beginning after picking up the sticker in the following level. You should already have the **Monkey Sticker** for the platform sticker switch next to the staircase that goes both ways, and if you took the time to bounce off the rubber snake toward the end of the previous level, you'll also have received the **Tiger Sticker** to slap onto the wall just after the first set of sliding stone platforms. Use the moving pillar to jump extra high to reach that ledge—the sticker will open up a secret hatch into the dangerous room next door.

Watch out for secret compartments in a few of the walls as well. In particular, the first challenge key is located in the wall right at the end of the large wave platform, just under the checkpoint, along with the **Large Wave Platform Object**, appropriately enough.

# The Temples:
## The Magician's Palace

Despite asking for your help, the cheeky Great Magician has decided to test your skills in his Temple of Emitters to see if you are up to the challenge of saving LittleBigPlanet. Are you? Of course you are. This is a sneaky level, filled with dissolving pathways and blocks that appear seemingly out of nowhere. Take your time to learn the patterns of the pathways before starting across to avoid an unexpected death, and be wary of being crushed by falling stones as you climb to the summit of the temple. After a few magic tricks from yourself, you'll soon be playing the Great Magician at his own game and will impress him enough for him to conjure up the exit to the level.

## Tricky Challenges

Slow and steady wins the race, and this level is surprisingly simple once you slacken the pace. Be sure to plan your jumps in advance and dawdle those extra few seconds before performing acrobatics to be certain that you aren't going to be surprised by a flurry of fire balls the moment you leap.

The hardest section is most likely the ascent to the summit of the temple via a hail of huge blocks. Be sure to always be standing on the tallest point to avoid being crushed by the next round of bricks.

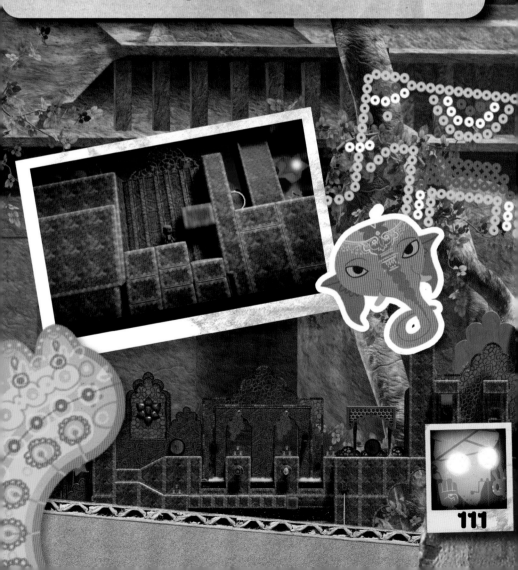

## Favorite Items

Everybody loves costumes—it's what makes our Sack People unique compared to our friends. And speaking of friends: Grab one to complete the two-player puzzle to the left of the summit of the big ascent section. Transport both players to the top of the tower using the buttons provided, and run along the top to grab tons of costume prize bubbles as well as the **New Delhi Dawn** Audio.

## Secret Gifts

If you can work out the Great Magician's magic box at the end of the level, grab the crate before it is substituted with something hotter and drag it over to the platform with the challenge key. Don't stop there—jump onto the magician's hand, then use the motion to leap onto his head and grab the **Great Magician's Magic Box Object**!

Near the beginning of the level is a rather simple secret area, during the particularly long vanishing blocks section. Use the tallest block to jump up and onto the back wall, then run around up there (including behind the window to the right) to find some prize bubbles.

Surprisingly, there is only one sticker switch in this level, but you'll need three stickers to complete it. Luckily, they're all pretty easy to find, so fill in the cobra outline above the two magic fabric-producing boxes to receive some costume items and the audio for the level.

# The Temples: Mini Levels

## The Shifting Temple

The challenge key for this level is found in a secret alcove at the end of the large wave section of the Elephant Temple. Run and jump through the temple to avoid being squashed and burned by the constantly shifting platforms. No matter how good you are, it will most likely take a few attempts to time the precise jumps needed to stay alive, so be sure to activate all the checkpoints as you reach them to avoid being sent back to the start. You might think it's a waste of time, but it could save you a few precious seconds in the long run.

## Pillar Jumping

The key for Pillar Jumping is easily spotted at the beginning of the mechanical elephant section of the Elephant Temple. A few simple jumps is all it takes to grab it.

A survival challenge this time—jump from pillar to pillar as they raise and lower into a gaseous pit to collect as many prize bubbles as possible. Always try and end up on the last pillar to rise and don't make any crazy leaps of faith. A short hop to the next pillar is all you should allow yourself.

## Fire Pits

The Great Magician's Temple holds the key to the Fire Pits on the ledge next to the magic box puzzle at the end of the level.

Navigate a maze in the bowels of the temple and complete two laps before the timer runs out. Sound easy? It's not. Grab as many prize bubbles as possible as you go, because you'll need to stop and start a lot to make each jump, especially across the ridiculously small platforms at the top of the circuit. Every platform in this level is designed to mess up the lazy jumper, so any mistakes will condemn you to a fiery death.

## THE COLLECTOR

### On to the Next Kingdom

Now that you've proved yourself to the Magician, it's time for the final battle. Navigate the harsh terrain of the spooky Wilderness and fight your way to the Collector's lair. LittleBigPlanet is depending on you to release his prisoners and defeat his gathering army, so there's no turning back now!

**THE COLLECTOR**

# The Wilderness:
# The Frozen Tundra

Upon entering the Frozen Tundra, you are immediately greeted by a rather battered bear. His family has been stolen by the Collector and you need to help him find them! Grab a dog sled and rocket through the Wilderness in search of the entrance to the evil mastermind's underground bunker. First you'll need to navigate the unstable, icy stalactites and stalagmites at the entrance to the cave before crashing through the army's first line of defense. Dodge the Collector's electrifying minions and a vicious pair of rocket launchers, then slide down the icy chasms to find a friendly face. This disillusioned soldier thinks the Collector has gone too far, and will lead you to the heart of the bunker . . .

## Tricky Challenges

Beware of falling icicles—those shards might help you climb to hard-to-reach platforms, but they can also crush you or knock any precarious platforms from beneath your feet!

Time your movements carefully when faced with the rocket launchers. If you do so, you'll easily manage to jump to the next alcove before the soldiers have time to reload.

On the final sliding descent—DON'T TOUCH THE CONTROLLER. Your momentum will automatically catapult you right into the arcs of prize bubbles.

## Favorite Items

You'll need to dress up warm to keep out the biting cold, so put on the big **Fur Hat** and **Great Coat Costumes** at the beginning of the level. If you think you're too tough to wrap up, though, complete the level to earn the **Robot Box Helmet**—the start of your transformation into a retro android!

You will need to play through this level several times to get all the prize bubbles, as there are often multiple paths to the same checkpoint, most of which will be inaccessible to backtracking. Take careful note of the icy platforms near the entrance to the cave especially, as there's something interesting on almost every one.

**The Wilderness**

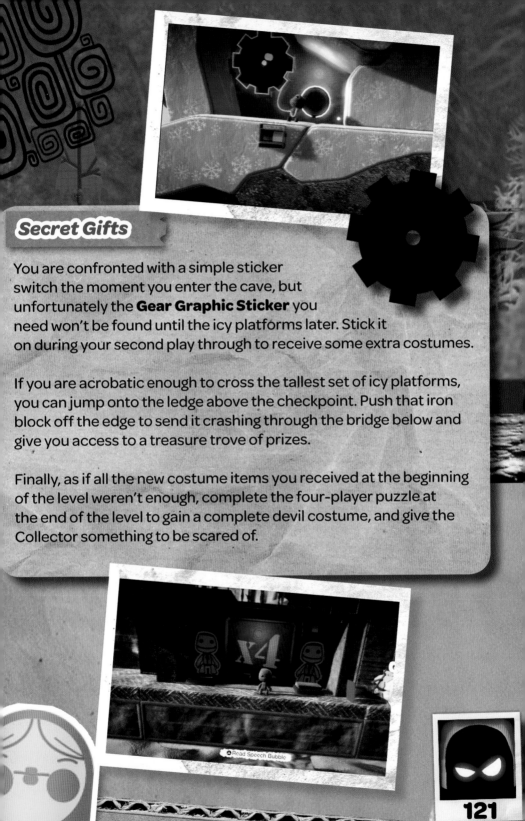

## Secret Gifts

You are confronted with a simple sticker switch the moment you enter the cave, but unfortunately the **Gear Graphic Sticker** you need won't be found until the icy platforms later. Stick it on during your second play through to receive some extra costumes.

If you are acrobatic enough to cross the tallest set of icy platforms, you can jump onto the ledge above the checkpoint. Push that iron block off the edge to send it crashing through the bridge below and give you access to a treasure trove of prizes.

Finally, as if all the new costume items you received at the beginning of the level weren't enough, complete the four-player puzzle at the end of the level to gain a complete devil costume, and give the Collector something to be scared of.

Read Speech Bubble

# The Wilderness: The Bunker

This is one of the hardest levels in the game and it's not going to get any easier! He might have let you into the compound, but the friendly soldier is far too scared to take you any farther, so it's up to you to navigate the electrifying obstacles as they attempt to block your route. Soon you'll be passing through rotating platforms and defeating shocking brain monsters. If you survive all of those challenges, you'll manage to rescue The Scientist. The Collector had been forcing him to make the creatures you've encountered—but not anymore. Finally, you'll have to navigate a huge spinning maze-wheel to reach the bottom of the bunker and move on to the Collector's lair.

# Tricky Challenges

It'd be silly to say *all of it*, but it's true, and you'll need to learn the entire level if you want to reach the end alive. In particular, though, the various spinning wheel obstacles are the toughest to navigate.

The pair of wheels with the corridors running through them are fairly simple to get across if you time it right—every other circuit will make them turn downward, throwing you into the electricity below, so be sure to jump the gap as the first one turns upward and then sprint for the end of the second one.

The wheel that takes you down onto the conveyor belt looks tough, with its shocking bars lining the interior. Use the lip of the entrance to jump onto a nearby snowdrift and simply walk over the top and down the other side to enter the wheel and go straight down.

The maze wheel is horrible, so remember that you are able to grab onto all of the fabric sections. Hold onto them as the wheel spins to time your movement to an outer ring. The last ring is the hardest and the trick is not to jump too far to the side to get from platform to platform—the speed of the wheel will often make you overshoot your target.

## Favorite Items

Play the Collector at his own game by earning the **Neon Wireframe Costume**—his creatures won't be the only ones that are shocking! Complete the level without dying (a near impossible task) to earn the matching helmet to go with it.

If you've taken a shine to those **Flip-Top Enemies**, springboard off the back of the first one to grab its prize bubble.

If you're going to get eggs, you might as well get free-range, which is why this chicken-friendly **Free-Range Egg Object** is so good for you! Grab it on the final conveyer belt before you finish the level.

**The Wilderness**

## Secret Gifts

Not so secret, more hard to reach—there are lots of opportunities to grab extra goodies if you decide to take a few risks! The best place to start is at those two rotating corridor wheels. Don't jump on them just yet—instead, move to the back plane behind the checkpoint and jump onto the snow drift. You'll be able to run along to the left to grab those prize bubbles you saw hiding behind the targets while you were dangling from the fabric ball a moment before.

Once you've passed the wheel section, immediately jump onto the snowdrift behind you. If you walk up the steep slope above the deadly puzzle, there is a sticker switch that uses the **Power Fist Sticker** you'll find in the next level. Then, move along that girder on the right to find a weird impact cannon and jump on the button a few times to blast a hole in the opposite wall to release even more prizes.

But wait, there's even more up there! Walk to the left and you'll find a weird, wheel-themed multiplayer puzzle. Two players can grab a nice collection of items from the puzzle, but to get the full haul you'll need a third.

125

# The Wilderness:
# The Collector's Lair

It's time for the final mission now: Releasing the citizens of LittleBigPlanet from the Collector's fiendish prison, which is powered by huge slabs of electricity.

You will have to descend into the heart of the structure to find the Bear family. Watch your step on the huge sliding slabs as you release Big Xam and Don Lu's dog. Some smaller platforms later, and King Croc and Zola are free.

Weird rotating corners challenge you next, but it's worth it to release Mags and Ze Dude. From there you'll have to manage your depth perception, as you move backward and forward through some quickly sliding chambers to release the Great Magician and Grandmaster Sensei.

Now you'll traverse the huge pistons for Frida and Don Lu, before the release of the Goddess signals the final descent into the underbelly of the prison. The King and Queen are there and celebrate your heroic deeds by throwing a huge parade of all the characters you've met on your journey. But it's not over yet; the Collector is still to come . . .

## Tricky Challenges

Be wary of momentum while on anything moving. There are a lot of easy ways to get squashed, so remember to adjust your movement to counter being thrown to the side by the sliding platforms.

When negotiating the rotating corners, remember that there is a piece of fabric on the inside of every one—use it to avoid getting thrown about too much!

It's worth making sure you release every creature. The more risks you take throughout the level to get every one, the more you're rewarded during the parade at the end of the level.

The final descent from the fabric ball and through the electrifying bowels of the prison is easier than it looks. Stay in the center of the screen to avoid almost all of the danger, and when you do eventually have to dodge around some obstacles, don't do it too early—it's actually safer to move at the last minute.

## Favorite Items

How can anybody fail to love the parade of items you receive at the end of the Lair? Now you can put all your favorite LittleBigPlanet characters into your own levels and continue the story with them!

If you've gotten this far, you're no doubt a skilled player at the game by now, so test your talent to the limit by completing the level without dying. You'll gain the **Neon Dress**, which goes with your helmet and costume to complete the outfit.

The epic audio to the level is pretty hard to reach and you'll have to time your jumps perfectly, while hanging from the small fabric ball in the right-angled platforms section of the level near Mags. Jump onto the platform as it swings beneath your feet, and jump again as it rotates once more to continue across. Practice makes perfect, and you'll also be rewarded with a challenge key if you manage to pull it off!

**The Wilderness**

## Secret Gifts

Most of the prize bubbles in this level are easily visible—the challenge is reaching them!

There is a sticker switch right at the beginning of the level. Jump over the hole in the ground before you descend to a small room on the right—if you place the **Wiry Tree Sticker** on the wall, you'll get a couple of fishy costume items!

Probably the most puzzling item is the **Tin Foil** material near the beginning of the level that seems to be locked inside its metal tube. You'll need to ask Don Lu's dog for one last favor if you want to get it out. After you release him, make your way back to the closed tube (a challenge in itself)—the dog will follow you underneath the platforms and once you get there its nose will hit a switch, allowing you access to the prize bubble.

# The Wilderness:
# The Collector

So begins the epic final battle. The diminutive Collector more than makes up for his short stature with his massive mechanical machines, and you'll have to defeat three distinct types before the creature is defeated.

The first has a simple hammering pattern—left, right, center—and it'll only take a moment to pop the two brains on either side. That said, it then proceeds to repeat the process but this time firing balls of electricity, which you'll have to dodge.

Moving up a level, you are confronted with a huge beast with giant fists that spews minions before pounding the ground. Get between its arms quickly to take out the majority of its brain bubbles in one go. You'll need to position yourself carefully to get the ones in the middle of its fists, though.

The final stage is a rather puny little box with electricity cannons on either side, which can bring balls of energy crashing down from the roof with each stamp. Once you've taken care of this final machine, you can give chase, finally cornering the Collector beneath his broken statue. He's been kidnapping people in an attempt to win friends—so he's not a bad man after all! It's not long before The King and Queen arrive, offering to share the world of LittleBigPlanet with him and work together to make it even better than it was before . . . and you can join them!

## Tricky Challenges

The quicker you do this, the easier it will be to defeat the Collector. Each repetition of the patterns gets more and more dangerous, so pop those brains as quickly as possible!

While the Collector is pounding the ground with those powerful robotic fists of his, remember the sumo you fought earlier in the game. Stay in close and try not to get thrown about by the motion of its arms.

During the final section, stay in the center of the machine. That way its electricity barrage won't touch you, and you can use the handy block that falls from the ceiling to jump onto its exposed center brain before it brings down another electrifying surprise.

# The Wilderness: Mini Levels

## Spline Rider

The challenge key for this level is underneath the second bridge in the Wilderness. When the jeep shoots out of the floor, jump down to pick it up.

Spline Rider is a more extreme version of Skateboard Freefall. Race down the icy mountainside as fast as you can to beat the timer, and hold on tight! Don't forget to hammer on the ✖ button whenever your sled is touching the ground for that extra boost of speed, particularly halfway through the level, where the quicker you go, the higher up the electrified section you'll get and the more prize bubbles you'll receive!

## Rotor Tubes

Remember those rotating corridor wheels in the Bunker level? Well, the challenge key for this level was in between them. That's essentially what you'll be doing as you race through this level to try and beat the timer. Remember that a well-timed jump can land you on the opposite side of the corridor as the wheel spins, so don't be afraid to hang around on one section while you watch for the pattern of the path up ahead. Just don't hit the electrified floor!

## Jetpack Tunnel

Find the challenge key just above the switch for Mags the Mechanic's cell in the Collector's Lair. You'll need to do some skillful acrobatics along the top of those shifting corner platforms to reach it, though!

Use your jetpack to stay alive for as long as possible in the electrified tunnel. The deadly floors and ceilings aren't your only worry, though, as there is also a large amount of poisonous gas ready for you to run into on either side of the screen if you don't keep your distance.

Take it slowly here and don't attempt to grab all the bubbles, as most of them are too close to the windy death-causing floor to be worth the effort. Stay near the top of the screen and pick up the easy points near the ceiling.

**The Wilderness**

## On to the Next Kingdom?

LittleBigPlanet might be safe, and the Collector might have turned out to be not quite such a meany after all, but there's still another kingdom to come and it holds the most exciting adventure of them all. An inspiring land of unlimited possibilities, exciting vistas, and fiendish puzzles, it's filled with items, objects, and materials from all the places in LittleBigPlanet you have visited so far. This handbook might not be able to help you as you explore this world, but we know that this next kingdom is going to be nothing short of spectacular!

And how do we know that?

Because the next kingdom is yours!

# Create!

It's time to show the population of LittleBigPlanet that it's not just they who can create exciting and entertaining worlds, it's you too! So travel to the Moon from your Pod and select a crater to begin building. You can start off by choosing a template for your level if you like—there's one for every kingdom you've unlocked in story mode, and it will provide you with a skeleton level to add things on to. But if you're feeling brave, you can leave it blank and build the whole thing from nothing!

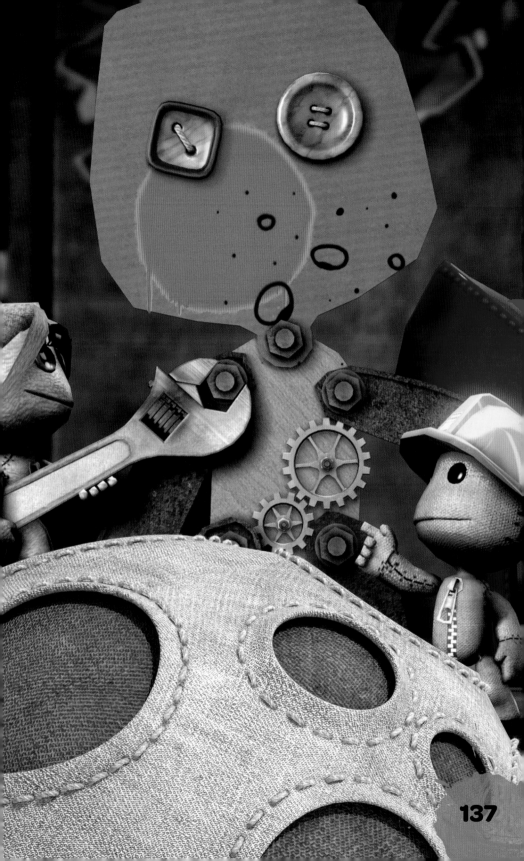

# Creation Controls

On top of all those nifty little tools you've been playing with during the story mode, the creation mode adds a whole host of extra abilities to your character to make designing your new levels as easy as flying.

What's that? Flying's not very easy? *Au contraire!* In creation mode, a simple press of the **[down on the D-pad]** button will transform you into hover mode! Using this, your Sack Person can float about the landscape anywhere he, or she, chooses. Use the left stick to move up, down, or side to side, and hold down the ❌ button to give yourself a little boost to get around quickly. The other buttons on the D-pad control time—up pauses (but leaves you free to work), left rewinds, and right fast-forwards—this helps you redo or undo any mistakes you might make!

The right stick also comes into its own now, as moving it backward can zoom out from the level to give you the chance to examine the structure in one go! Use it to look at the whole picture and then zoom in to examine the finer details.

You might also notice that there is a thermometer on the side of the screen—this shows you how much more stuff you can fit into the level, so keep an eye on it!

Those might be cool gadgets, but the best is yet to come, as we examine the brand-new features of your Popit menu!

# The Popit Cursor

The Popit cursor is a very useful tool to use while editing. Once selected, simply move it around the world and press the ⊗ button to grab hold of something. Once you've picked it up you can move it around the world as much as you like, and even change its depth with **[L1]** and **[L2]** and rotate or scale it with the right stick. If you press the ⊗ button again, the object will stay suspended in space while you continue to work. But be warned: When you press the back button it will fall to the ground once more—that is, unless you've created something to hold it in position!

If you have second thoughts about what you've △ created, you can always delete it by pressing the button while it is selected to send it packing to your goodies bag.

# The Goodies Bag

Ever wondered where all those lovely prize bubbles ended up after you popped them in the story mode? Well, here's where!
Opening it up will reveal four windows. The first, Materials, contains all the different textures and, well, materials, you've picked up along the way. You'll find out in a minute how to use them to create the groundwork for your level. The second window is Collected Objects, and contains all the gadgets and contraptions you've encountered on your travels. You might not be able to use them to build a wall, but building a wall from a giant football doesn't sound like a good idea, anyway—besides, there are many other exciting properties you can give objects. The third window contains My Objects, ones that you've created and stored for use later. The fourth and final window is Community Objects, and features the contraptions other Sack People have built and felt so proud of that they've left them in a prize bubble in their level for you to pick up and use yourself. How generous!

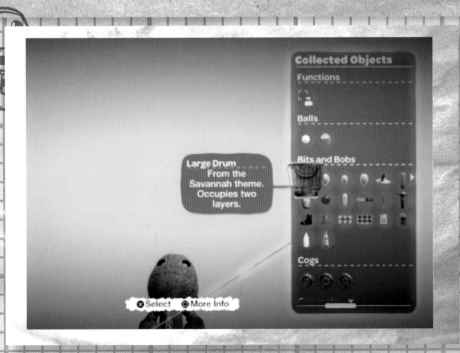

**Create!**

# *Materials*

These materials act as the basic building blocks for your level. Simply select them from your Popit, then choose a basic shape for you to begin your building. From there, you can use the Popit cursor tools to change depth, size, and rotation. **[R1]** and **[R2]** will also change the thickness of your object, so you can span all three planes.

You don't have to keep everything as a circle, square, triangle, or any other basic shape, though; holding down the action button ✕ will let you drag the shape across the air. Or overlapping two objects on the same plane will cause them to merge, even if they're different materials!

The delete button △ acts as a cutting tool; simply select the shape you want the hole in your material to be, then press the △ button to cut it out of the object.

# Glue

Glue is a very useful tool and extremely easy to use. If you've created two objects that would be much more useful as one, simply pick one up with the cursor and hold it touching the second object. If you keep the ✖ button pressed, there will be a pop and the two objects will have magically joined! This even works when the shapes are on differing planes, as long as they're touching, and can be used to anchor trees and characters firmly to the ground.

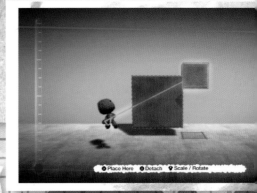

# Special Materials

Floaty Material will either float in one place (like the **Pink Floaty**) or even float away if not tethered (like the **Peach Floaty**).

**Glass** is slippery and tough, so keep your jumping precise while moving on it.

**Rubber** has tons of grip, which is why it's so good when used to make tires.

**Dark Matter** is immovable and will stay suspended wherever you've placed it, even when the gravity has been turned back on.

**Dissolvable Material** is capable of disappearing when triggered, but we'll get to things like "triggers" later . . .

**Create!**

# Collected Objects

Here is where all the fancy objects you've collected on your journey through LittleBigPlanet are stored. If you've been dreaming of a level where you have to push a football through a maze to slot it into a high-heeled shoe, here is where you need to go!

If you've managed to finish the story, you should have quite a few gadgets, creatures, and characters in your Goodies Bag. You'll notice when you place them in your world that the ■ button will appear if you hold your cursor over the object. This means you can change the settings on mechanical objects, such a piston's speed, length, and strength, and you can also synchronize it with other objects in the world. If it's a character, you canalso add a speech bubble by pressing ■ on its mouth.

If you're wondering why the cogs you've discovered won't stick to walls or interlock with each other, don't worry. You'll discover the means to attach things together, change the properties of an object or material, and even instil intelligence into a creature in the Tool Bag section of this handbook. In the meantime, don't be afraid to use the creatures, devices, and characters you've already gained. We don't all have the time to start creating complex machines from scratch—it takes practice and hard work!

# Community Objects

This is where the other Sack People of LittleBigPlanet come in. They've taken the time and effort to create their own levels, and also their own objects, items, and monsters. By playing their levels, you will receive prize bubbles containing their hard work for you to access here. LittleBigPlanet's world is all about sharing, so don't be afraid to use an item that someone else has made if you realize that it's perfect for your level. But credit where credit's due—don't forget to go back and give them a nice rating for all their hard work, and who knows, soon you might be able to create something for *them* to use in return!

## My Objects

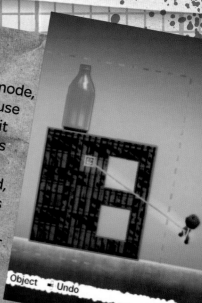

When you first start in the creation mode, this menu won't appear. That's because you'll need to learn about how to use it in the Tool Bag in the next section. This is where all the nifty shapes and items you'll create in this mode can be stored, and is how all those community objects were captured for your use. Simply use the Capture Object tool to highlight your creations and they will then be stored here for use as many times as you want, wherever you want! Neat, eh?

# The Tool Bag

Okay, so we've got our materials and our objects, and we know how to resize, reshape, and place them into our level. It's a great start, but now it's time to open the Tool Bag and begin to make things a little more complicated.

In this section you will learn how to fine-tune the objects you've created and create living monsters and traps, as well as change the environment and mood of your level by adding audio objects, backgrounds, and even changing the time of day or night! Let's get started.

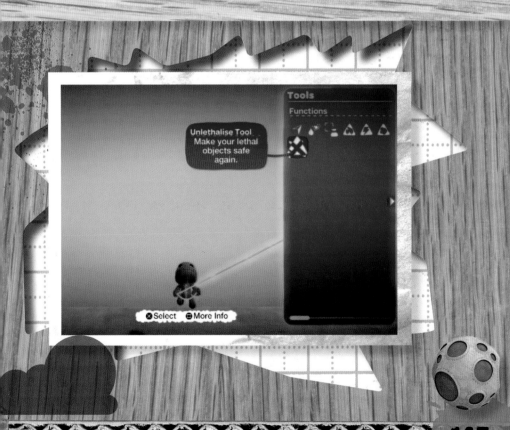

# The Corner Tool

You can use the corner tool to tweak the material shapes that you have already made in the world. Simply select the icon and move the cursor over the shape you want to edit. By pressing ⊗ you will find that the cursor becomes stuck to the edges of the object, and by holding down the ⊗ you can drag those corners into or out of the shape. Remember you can press △ at any time to undo any mistakes.

# The Capture Object Tool

As mentioned in the previous section, this tool will let you grab anything you've created to use at any time. Select this tool, then

use the adjustable box to highlight the object you want to store and press ⊗. When you next go to your Goodies Bag, you'll find the item stored in your My Objects page. The tool icon will also appear in the Goodies Bag pages to make it even easier to use.

**Create!**

## Lethalizing and Unlethalizing

You'll find some nasty danger tools in your Tool Bag as well. Using these, you can convert any object in your world into something deadly. It might be the Electricity Tool, the Flame Tool, or the Horrible Gas Tool—either way, no Sack Person is going to survive an encounter with these!

If you change your mind and decide to be a nice creator, simply use the Unlethalizer Tool to convert the object back to its original form.

## The Material Changer

Select this icon, choose the material you want to change in the object you've made, and use the cursor to substitute it. Simple as that!

# Gadgets

It's alive! It's alive, I tell you! Or at least your level will be after you've used these gadgets!

## Connectors

Connectors comprise the basic mechanical elements of everything in LittleBigPlanet and there's quite a selection to choose from.

The first group are Bolts, and these will connect one object to another. Either stick a bolt in the first object you want to attach, then glue it to the other object, or hold both objects together to put a bolt through both! There are four different types—a regular Bolt, a Wobble Bolt (which will make an object wobble), a Sprung Bolt that will wobble but return to its original position, and a motorized bolt which will spin around. You can adjust the speed and tightness of a Bolt in the tweak menu, as well as the angle.

Then there are the other connectors: strings, rods, elastic rods, springs, winches, and pistons, which all do exactly what their names suggest. Connect both ends to the two objects you want to join and adjust the properties available for each type!

**Create!**

## *Creature Pieces*

Whether you're building a helpful dog or an evil enemy, these are the building blocks of all the creatures in LittleBigPlanet. Make sure that they have something to move about with for a start, and then add eyes and a mouth so that they can interact. Finally, you'll need to add a creature brain—these can be protected or unprotected, but unprotected creatures are open to attack from other Sack People! The tweak menu for these brains has a huge amount of things you can customize—whether they follow the player or run away, how fast they move, whether they can jump and how high, and if they are indestructible or not.

You can also set limits on where your creature can move by adding Creature Navigators to your level. When it approaches one of these, the beast will automatically change direction—handy for stopping your evil monster from falling into a fiery pit before the player has a chance to foil them!

# Special

You'll notice you have a couple of Special items in your gadgets section, and both of them create some very interesting gameplay possibilities.

The Emitter does exactly what it sounds like it does—it emits things. You can choose what object it emits, where it emits it, and at what speed and rotation the object is fired out at. You can also put a limit on how many it emits at once and how many in total, as well as how long the emitted objects last. You don't want to swamp your level with a million footballs in half a minute, do you?

There is also the Rocket object. Attach this to something and it will thrust it in whichever direction you've decided. You can adjust the power and decide whether it stays on or off. You might want to leave any rockets you place in the "off" position for now, because next we'll be looking at switches!

**Create!**

# Switches

Switches are brilliant and will form the basis of all the brilliant puzzles you'll no doubt be challenging visiting Sack People with in your level!

When you place a switch, you'll need to drag the little green wire that sprouts from it over to the mechanical device you want it to affect. Once those are connected, you can tweak the switch to determine what you want it to achieve, whether it be to start a motor or piston, stop it, make it move faster, or reverse its motion—anything, really. And with three-way switches you have even more options! With the sticker switch, don't forget to set a sticker to correspond to it, and with the magnetic switch you'll need to stick a magnetic key to something else that is moving toward it to trigger the switch when it approaches. You can change the color of the magnetic keys to avoid confusion on different puzzles.

# Gameplay Kits

The Gameplay Kits menu adds a touch of the theatrical to your level and you'll be able to fine-tune how each section looks and feels from the player's perspective.

# Basic Kit

The basic kit contains all the fundamental elements for creating a level and you'll need to use nearly all of them if you want to build a complete experience for other Sack People.

You will, of course, need an Entrance and a Scoreboard so that players can start and finish the level, but Checkpoints and Double-Life Checkpoints will also be needed to stop any frustration. There's nothing worse than completing a difficult section only to be sent right back to the beginning the next time you die! You can add rewards to the scoreboard using the tweak menu, so don't forget to give players a little treat for doing particularly well!

A Close-Level Post will also stop other players from joining the game halfway through. You don't want them to miss all those lovely opening puzzles you spent so long creating, do you?

Score Bubbles and Prize Bubbles are also a good incentive for players to explore all the nooks and crannies in a level, and to keep coming back to try and solve all those puzzles you've hidden prizes in! The tweak menu lets you choose which items to store in the prize bubbles and you can set them to private or shareable. Try putting some of the best objects you've created inside a few of the bubbles to show off your creations!

As well as the gameplay-related items, there are also a couple of camera ones. The Camera Zone lets you adjust the position of the camera in a certain section of the level, making it swing around to show the player that giant flaming boulder that's chasing them, for example. Use the tweak menu to adjust the zoom, tracking, and angle of the camera.

Obviously, when you and your friends play through your shiny new creation, you'll want a souvenir. That's when the Photo Booth function comes into effect. Place it on an object and set the timer and position of the camera to catch a mid-action snapshot or a posed group picture!

## Character Enhancements

The only character enhancement you'll find in the story mode will be the jetpack, but it's a useful tool for adding an extra height dimension to your puzzles. However, there are some more accessories available in the LittleBigPlanet store. Look around at some of the user-created content for a sneak peek at them being used in other levels!

# Dangerous

Creating fire pits and other dangerous obstacles might be fun, but these vicious pieces of equipment are guaranteed to shake things up even more. Beware of spikes and impact. You'll no doubt have encountered a few of them on your journey through the story. Trigger explosives, however, are more interesting—hook them up to a switch to make them explode. There's nothing more frightening for a player than running through an environment that's gradually being demolished by proximity triggers!

# Racing

If you think a level you have made might be a bit too easy, try making your players beat it against the clock! Grab a start gate and place it on the map (remember, as with stickers, you can click the right stick to flip it around), then place some finish posts at the other end of the section you want to race along. Tweaking the start posts will let you adjust how much time the level has to be beaten in, so be careful: Make it too long and it won't make a difference, too short and your players might get a little frustrated—so test it out yourself first!

# Audio Objects

This section of the Tool Bag can really bring your levels to life, and soon your players won't be able to resist tapping their feet in time to the music or laughing at a ridiculous noise!

# Music

Choose a music object from the menu (hopefully you'll have collected quite a few on your travels) and place it in the world like you would any other object. But this time you can use the tweak menu to really customize the music! Press the ■ button while the cursor is hovering over the music player, and you can choose the volumes of the individual instruments and at what point in the song it will start playing from. You can also adjust the radius of how close your Sack Person needs to be to trigger the start of the music. To make the experience even more of a pleasant surprise for the player, you can also make the music object invisible. Not all tracks are as tweakable as others, and only ones in the Music-Interactive section allow you to manipulate the balance of the songs.

# Sound Objects

To place a sound effect in the world, select it and place it on the object you want to make the noise. There are a menagerie of sounds to choose from and you can find them in the tweak menu. From there, you can also adjust the pitch of the noise, the reason for it triggering (player proximity, switch trigger, impact trigger, or destruction), and its visibility.

# Backgrounds and Global Controls

The last two pages in the Tool Bag contain the Backgrounds and Global Controls. These tools transport your level to a completely different setting and hopefully you'll have picked up some backgrounds during your travels through the story mode.

The Islands Background scenery from "The Islands" theme.

Once you've chosen a background, though, that doesn't mean you've finished. Scroll across one more time to the Global Controls Menu. Here you can fine tune your environment even more, changing day to night and adjusting the darkness. You can also add fog (which you can adjust the color of), and sliding the color correction bar can change the screen to sepia, black and white, soft focus, and a load of other variations in between!

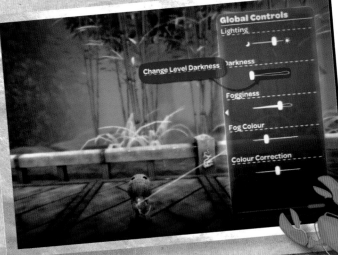

Change Level Darkness

Global Controls
Lighting
Darkness
Fogginess
Fog Colour
Colour Correction

# *The Pause Menu*

The Popit menu isn't the only one to have a few additions. Now that we've made a few objects, let's take a look at the Pause Menu's new features:

**Grid Options**—Switch these on to make sure everything is lined up correctly.

**View**—If you've changed the camera on your level to something more dynamic, here you can flip between the zoomed-in game view mode and the more flexible editing view.

**About My Level**—Here you can add a description, title, and even choose an icon for your level.

**Save Level/Save Level As**—You can choose to save your level in your original landing spot or move it elsewhere on the moon.

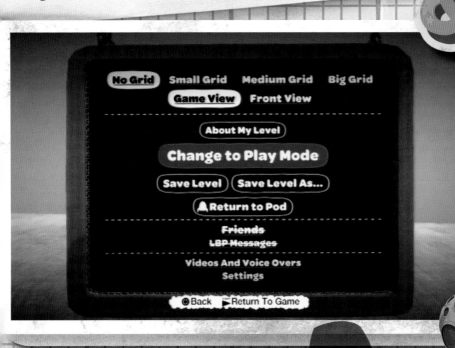

# Putting It All Together

So our Goodies Bag is bursting at the seams, we've completed all the tutorials (did you notice all the extra prizes we got for those?), and we've played with all the gadgets, gizmos, materials, and objects offered. Now it's time to get started and make our own level!

Over the next few pages we'll show you how to make a short, simple level using all the skills we've learned in this section. You can either use it as a skeleton to add more puzzles and traps to, or simply as an introduction, continuing the level on even further until that thermometer is bubbling hot! If you're feeling really confident, you could decide not to use it at all and instead look at the tricks we've used to create the traps, puzzles, and characters to spin off into a whole new direction. That is, after all, what LittleBigPlanet is all about: Doing your own thing!

Remember: Don't be afraid to replay any of the tutorial videos from the Start Menu as you go along if you can't remember how to do something—that's what they're there for.

**Create!**

# Setting the Scene

First we go to My Moon. As it's only a short level we'll be making, we choose a small crater and dive in with a blank template.

It all looks a bit bland at the moment, so let's create an inspiring canvas to work on. Choose the Gardens background in Tools and set the lighting to early morning. Put the color correction in the middle for a magical, sepia-tinged glow, and we're ready to start!

Let's put the basics in first. We have an Entrance already, but put in a Close-Level Post a little way to the right, and in between let's add The Queen from our Goodies Bag (or another character if you don't have her) to welcome our players to this adventure. Add a dramatic cut scene angle and put a nice welcome message into her speech bubble: "Hello, welcome to my first LittleBigPlanet level!"

# The First Obstacle

Okay, it's time to add a bit of a challenge. In the back plane, use the oval shape to make a small ceramic hillock—a cartoon cloud-shape that will take a few seconds for the Sack Person to run past. About two-thirds in, in front of this, we'll add a thick box, too tall for the player to reach without help. Now, let's give him or her some help! Use the standard cube shape to place a foam block just after the Close-Level Post and before the hillock, so the player can drag this over to the ledge to get over it!

Not much of a challenge, though, is it? So insert a foam rectangle right in the middle of the big ceramic box we've made. Leave plenty of room on either side for the Sack Person to stand comfortably. Now go into the Tools Bag and set fire to it! To cheer the player up after navigating this challenge, plop five score bubbles on the downward curving side of the hillock, to reward them after they've crossed the fire.

Now for the final atmospheric touches. Glue two or three trees onto the hillock so that cheeky players can't just run up and over it to avoid solving the puzzle, and maybe go back and put one next to The Queen to keep her happy. Finally, put some music on the front of the hillock just before the large ceramic block, adjust the sounds to your taste, and set a small trigger radius—the music should kick in just as the Sack Person pushes the block past it!

**Create!**

# Switcheroo

It's time for a proper puzzle now, and to the right of the base of the ceramic hillock we'll put a soccer ball! Make sure it's small enough for the player to jump over if it's not their thing, but if they feel like dribbling it along the level a little bit, they're in for a treat!

A fair distance away, put a pair of tall, thin trees side by side—one on the farthest plane and one on the nearest. These are our goalposts (make sure you stick them down—we don't want them to go flying when the player scores!). Grab an emitter from your Tools Bag and place it in the branches of one of the trees, set the emission source just above and to the right of the tree, and tweak it to produce fifteen score bubbles instantaneously, with a lifespan of ten seconds.

Also in the tree, add a magnetic switch and wire it to the emitter. Make sure the trigger radius reaches across the ground a little way and have it set to "on/off." Now, go back to the soccer ball and place the trigger key on it. Make sure all the switches and emitters are invisible and now you're set! When the player dribbles the ball to the goalposts, it will trigger the emitter and shower them with score bubbles!

# Halftime Break

Time for a Checkpoint we reckon, so build a small grassy knoll at the back of the level and stick a Checkpoint onto it. Then grab Humpty from the characters section of your Goodies Bag (if you didn't find Humpty, any character will do) and place him next to the knoll. Type in the speech bubble: "Watch out! Weedkiller has spilled onto the path ahead!" What is he talking about? We'll soon find out.

On your travels you should have picked up a **Large Oak Tree** scenic object. Place a couple of these close together just after Humpty. They are very large so leave them that way for the moment. Then take a similar patterned fabric to the trees and, using the circle tool, make a double depth thick pathway linking the two sets of branches to make it easier for the player to cross once they get up there!

Below the trees, grab some more fabric and create a one-box-high, three-levels-deep carpet running from the center of the trunk of one tree to the other. Using the Lethalizing Tool, convert this fabric into Horrible Gas! Now we have our weedkiller. Put some semi-circular grass fabric boundaries on either side, so the player won't walk into it accidentally!

Create!

## Acrobatics

We have our dangerous pathway and our safe route through the Large Oak Trees, but how do we get up there? We're going to have to make our first fancy contraption!

Using a Motorized Bolt, pin a circular ball of fabric to the front of the left-hand ball of "leaves" on the tree. Set the motor to full power and a fairly quick speed. Using the pause function so that they stay in position, place three similar balls around the central motor and connect them with *stiff* rods. Finally, adjust the length of each rod so that they are all the same distance from the center, but also so that they will swing close enough to the ground for a Sack Person to easily jump and grab them as they pass. Then set the rods to invisible.

Now would be a good time to test your level in Play Mode. It should be easy to use the fabric balls to swing up into the tree branches and walk across the tops to the other side, out of harm's way. Stick some prize bubbles on there, as well as on the bottom of each rotating fabric ball, to reward our plucky players!

## Scaring the Dog!

Add another Humpty at the end of the tree section and place a Checkpoint in the wall at his feet. He needs another speech bubble now, so type: "Phew, you made it! Now race my dog in the flying saucer I made." Flying Saucer? Dog? It looks like we have work to do.

To create the dog, make a fairly large semicircle of dog-colored fabric and suspend it in the air, add two or three wheels from the Creature Components section, and an eye (if you're feeling really fancy you can add a dog sound-effect as well!). Finally, add a creature brain—set it to "flee" with a large trigger radius and maximum speed, so that when the player approaches, it starts running as fast as it can!

**Create!**

Next, we need the flying saucer. Sadly, Humpty can't make one that actually flies, so we'll have to make do. In the middle plane, make a flat oval of metal that can be easily jumped onto and bolt large rollerskate wheels to both ends. Next, attach a small triangle of fabric and on the back stick a large rocket with medium boost. This is looking to be some car! Create the starting mechanism by linking a switch you can grab to the rocket and we're ready to race.

## The Course

Next, we need to build a course for them to race along. Just before where we've placed the two vehicles (and just after Humpty and the Checkpoint) insert some starting posts, changing the time limit to twenty or thirty seconds. Scroll along the level a reasonable distance with some finishing posts, and plonk them down with a grassy knoll to the right, to give your "flying saucer" a soft landing!

So far the race track is a bit dull, so let's liven it up a bit. How about an impenetrable wall across the middle of the track? Sound stupid? How about if it's made of Dissolvable Material? Build a small ramp leading up to it out of grass fabric and place a magnetic switch near the beginning of the ramp, connected to the wall. Place the corresponding key onto the middle of your flying saucer. Now the player won't be able to progress without trying out your funky vehicle to dissolve the wall.

Finally, for the last stretch before the finish, add a variety of Trigger Explosives spaced just far enough apart so as not to trigger one another, and place proximity switches on each one except for the first. Don't wire them up to their own explosives, though; instead attach each to the one *before*—this will create a ripple of explosions that won't harm the player, but will certainly make them jump! Place a final proximity switch for the final explosive on the finishing line for a spectacular finish.

**Create!**

# And Finally

To finish let's add a scoreboard, set to reward the player with an object for finishing the level and another one for acing it. We've decided to put our dog and flying saucer objects in there ourselves, but you might have created something even more spectacular you want to show off.

Of course, this doesn't mean that *you* have to finish the level here. Even on the smallest crater the thermometer is only half full. Continue the adventures of Humpty and his dog, or simply expand the level we've made. Add some rolling hills to race across in your car, or some swinging foam balls to traverse the deadly weedkiller—and we haven't even begun to add menacing wildlife to the garden!

Take as long as you like to make your level the best it can be, and when you've finished it, tested it, and saved it with its own unique name and icon, you'll be ready to put it online for all the other Sack People on LittleBigPlanet to enjoy!

# Share!

Okay, so you've saved LittleBigPlanet, you've created your own levels on My Moon . . . What else is there to do?

Share it with all the other Sack People in the LittleBigPlanet universe, of course!

This chapter will give you some information on how to interact with all the other friendly Sack People across the world. It will show you how to upload and share levels, play other people's, and travel with a friend through the various kingdoms you've unlocked to grab all those two- to four-player goodies you spotted on your first time around.

# Other Sack People

There are lots of other Sack People who are playing LittleBigPlanet around the world, and as you meet them you'll discover all kinds of weird and wonderful personalities. From outlandish dress sense to fiendishly complex level designs, use these fellow players to inspire your own creations. If you're lucky, they might have left some of the designs that they're particularly proud of lying around their levels, so if you want a jet ski but don't know how to make one, go and find someone who does! It's guaranteed that you'll stumble across all kinds of objects and situations that will make you think: "I didn't know you could do *that*!" Because after all, the only limit in LittleBigPlanet is your imagination.

**Share!**

## Online Etiquette and Safety

When playing online, remember to be as polite as you would be if you were talking to your grandma. No swearing, rudeness, or rude drawings—we want to make all the Sack People in LittleBigPlanet get along like one big happy family.

Like anything else on the Internet, you need to stay safe. Be careful when talking to people you've never met before—you never know who could turn out to be a Nasty Nigel. And don't use your real name when playing—your profile and avatar pictures allow you to choose whatever wacky and crazy title you want to call yourself, so take advantage of it!

# Playing Together Online

Playing the story mode with others is very simple. If you are connected to the PlayStation Network, you will be able to see how many people are playing, whichever level you are looking at. All you need to do then is to press "Play Online" on your menu to jump into a game with them.

The first person to enter the level becomes the host and any other players will automatically follow them to their Pod once that level has been completed.

If the host decides to go to a different level, the other players will automatically follow them. But if a non-host player decides to leave, the option will come up to follow them instead.

Use the Start Menu and go to "player management" to see who you are currently following.

You can also play the levels offline with a friend if you have an extra controller—their Sack Person will join you as soon as it is switched on (as long as you haven't passed a Close-Level Post!). Choose "play on your own" to keep the level local!

**Share!**

# Multi-Player Puzzles

The big draw of playing with friends is that you can access all those areas that one Sack Person alone can't. Look out for the x2, x3, and x4 signs scattered throughout most of the levels to find a puzzle that can only be solved by working together. Some of them might be hidden away so you'll need to make sure you explore every inch! Use the handy text chat button in your Popit to send messages to your fellow players to help organize yourselves.

## The Close-Level Post

Make sure you've gathered all your friends before you begin the level, as all of them have a Close-Level Post just after the opening checkpoint. Once you've passed this marker no one else is allowed into your game. This means you won't suddenly encounter a crowd of people halfway through, but also that you'll need to make sure you have all your fellow players with you before you begin.

# Publishing Your Levels

My Moon might be a fun place to run around in, but it'll get lonely after a while if you don't send all your new levels out into the big wide world for others to play and enjoy!

To share a level, find the crater you want to publish on the moon and select "publish." Make sure you've named the level and added a description to help other players know what it is before they try it, then change the icon that represents it so that it will stand out from the crowd.

Once published, your level can be played, rated, and described by all the other Sack People, so make sure it's the most fun and exciting adventure you can possibly make!

**Share!**

## Playing Other Users' Levels

Just like you, there are millions of other players creating their own levels and putting them out there for you to play. While looking at LittleBigPlanet, scroll down to the community section of the menu. Entering that will take you to a selection of the most recently published levels for you to see, or you can search for levels by creator, description, rating, most-hearted, or busiest. Once you've completed one level by a creator, you will be asked to rate and describe it. After that, you'll be shown all of his, or her, other creations—if you liked what you played, you might want to check them out!

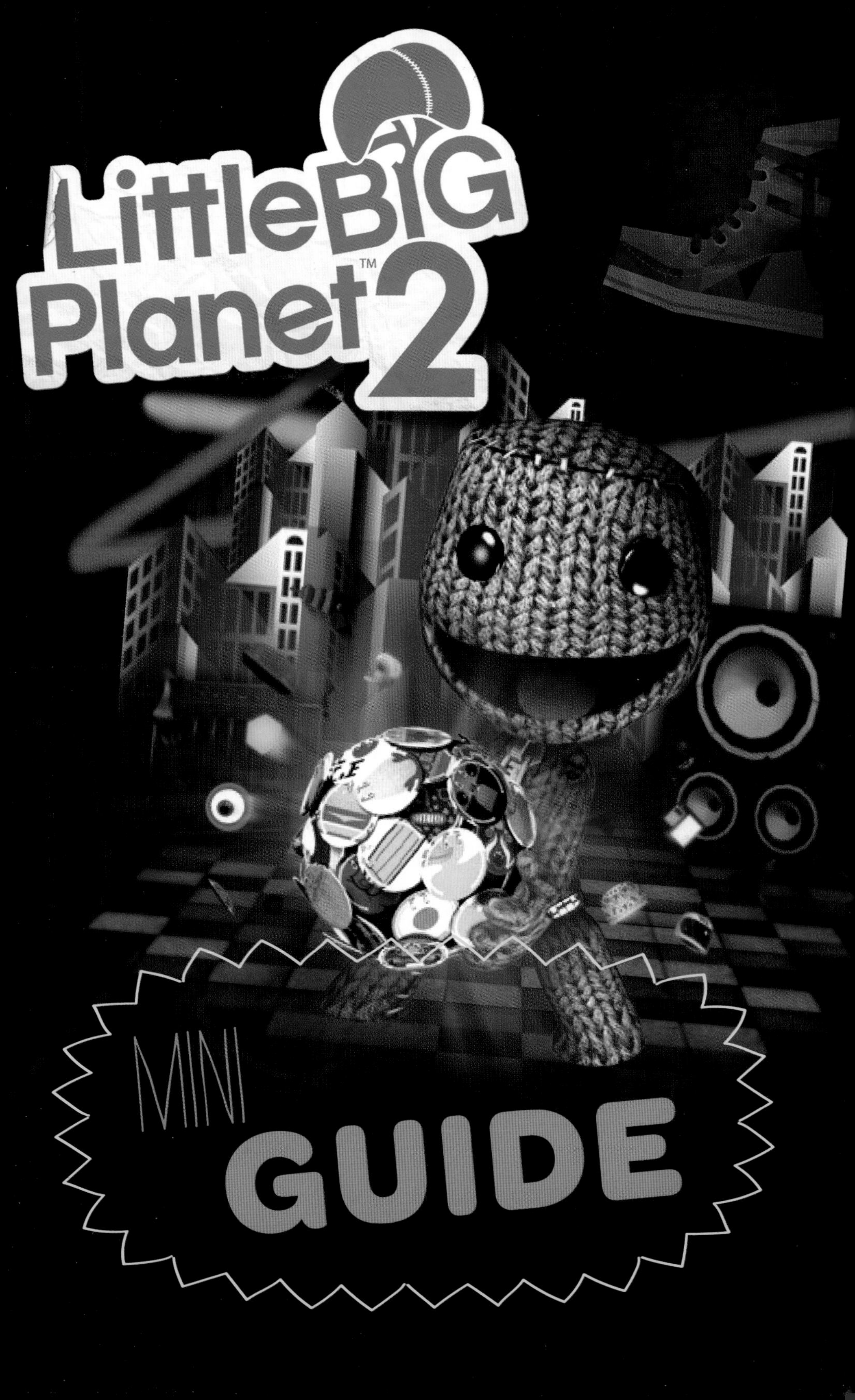
LittleBIG Planet™ 2
MINI
GUIDE

# Craftworld Is in Peril!

Your Sackboy's gentle stroll through the idyllic landscape of Craftworld (and past its Creators, the friendly developers at Media Molecule) is rudely interrupted by a mysterious and deadly force. A giant vacuum cleaner is tearing apart the world! Luckily, you are rescued in the nick of time by a mysterious inventor named Larry Da Vinci.

He tells you of the evil Negativitron that has enslaved Craftworld and corrupted its people. Larry Da Vinci is the joint leader of the Alliance—a resistance group dedicated to freeing the people of LittleBigPlanet once more.

Together with Da Vinci, you embark on a journey to free the other members of the Alliance and construct an army to defeat the Negativitron. Your epic quest takes you from cake-filled kingdoms to dark factories, and even beyond Craftworld itself. Have you got what it takes to guide Sackboy safely through his weird and wondrous adventures to save the world?

Yes?

THEN WHAT ARE YOU WAITING FOR ?

# And that's not even the half of it...

It's easy to link camera changes (or even trigger the movements of your Sackbots) during cutscenes, but if you're feeling really brave you can also put the music in charge of an entire level! Try creating sections of path that all link to an emitter, then tie each section to a different element of the music—as the track progresses, the level will put itself together in front of you!

This trick even works in reverse. Use Holographic Material to make new collectibles and link each one to a different note or instrument. Depending on which collectibles a player collects and in what order, a different tune will be produced each time—truly a musical miracle!

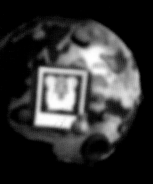

# AND REMEMBER . . .

It's easy to get excited about the new world of possibilities in LittleBigPlanet™ 2, but spare a thought for your prized creations back in the first LittleBigPlanet™. Over three million levels have been made by people like you, and it would be a shame to just forget about them—so that's why they have come along with you!

Yes, all those levels you and your friends created are still there for you to experience all over again, and they're looking better than ever! Who knows, you may even find that some of the new tools available to you will change those old levels beyond recognition.

## YOU HELPED MAKE THIS WORLD,

## AND DON'T YOU FORGET IT!